PHILOTUS;

A

COMEDY.

REPRINTED FROM THE EDITION OF

ROBERT CHARTERIS.

EDINBURGH:

PRINTED BY BALLANTYNE AND COMPANY.

M.DCCC.XXXV.

THE BANNATYNE CLUB.

M.DCCC.XXXV.

THOMAS THOMSON, ESQ.

PRESIDENT.

HON. HENRY COCKBURN, LORD COCKBURN. VICE-
PRESIDENT.

DAVID CONSTABLE, ESQ.

ANDREW COVENTRY, ESQ.

JAMES T. GIBSON CRAIG, ESQ. TREASURER

WILLIAM GIBSON CRAIG, ESQ.

HON. GEORGE CRANSTOUN, LORD COREHOUSE.

THE EARL OF DALHOUSIE.

JAMES DENNISTOUN, ESQ.

GEORGE DUNDAS, ESQ.

ROBERT DUNDAS, ESQ.

RIGHT HON. W. DUNDAS, LORD CLERK REGISTER.

CHARLES FERGUSSON, ESQ.

ROBERT FERGUSON, ESQ.

GENERAL SIR RONALD C. FERGUSON.

COUNT MERCER DE FLAHAULT.

HON. JOHN FULLERTON, LORD FULLERTON.

THE DUKE OF GORDON.

WILLIAM GOTT, ESQ.

ROBERT GRAHAM, ESQ.

LORD GRAY.

RIGHT HON. THOMAS GRENVILLE.

LORD HOLLAND.

THE EARL OF HADDINGTON.

THE DUKE OF HAMILTON AND BRANDON.

EDW. W. A. DRUMMOND HAY, ESQ.

SIR JOHN HAY, BART.

JAMES MAITLAND HOG, ESQ.

THE BANNATYNE CLUB.

PREFACE.

In the scanty annals of the early Scotish drama, the comedy of Philotus occupies a very conspicuous place. It is therefore a subject of some regret that the name of the poet has not hitherto been ascertained; for there is no evidence, and indeed no great probability, of its having been written by Robert Semple, who has sometimes been represented as the author. He is mentioned as the writer of a play, which on the 17th of January 1568 was acted before the regent and others of the nobility;[1] and it has been taken for granted that he was the writer of Philotus, which has not been appropriated by any other author. Various plays were however written and acted which were never printed, and which are no longer preserved in manuscript; nor must we so rapidly hasten to the conclusion, that this particular drama could only be the composition of an individual who is recorded as the writer of some drama, unnamed and undescribed.

[1] Birrel's Diary, p. 14, in Dalyell's Fragments of Scotish History. Edinb. 1798, 4to.

On evidence equally doubtful, several writers have represented this poet as a Scotish peer.[1] The evidence indeed amounts to little more than this:—the fourth Lord Semple bore the same name, and after the year 1570 the poet changed his signature to Semple. The identity of the name is itself a very slender proof, and requires no particular consideration. In Bannatyne's MS. he appears as Semple, without the addition of his Christian name; but if this circumstance is to be admitted as evidence, Dunbar, Henryson, Scott, and various other poets may in the same manner be elevated to the dignity of the peerage. Lord Semple succeeded his grandfather in 1572,[2] and the manuscript was written in 1568: it is evident that at this latter date Robert Semple was not a peer, though we find him here mentioned by his surname. In the Legend of the Bishop of Sanctandrois Lyfe, which, as it mentions Adamson's journey to London, must have been written so late as the year 1583, the author describes himself by his initials R. S. It is admitted that Lord Semple continued to profess the popish religion; but the poems of Robert Semple contain the most unequivocal proofs of having been written by a protestant, and the Legend was manifestly written by a zealous presbyterian. According to

[1] Sibbald's Chronicle of Scottish Poetry, vol. iii. p. 397. Preface to Semple's Sege of the Castel of Edinburgh. [Lond. 1813] 4to. Motherwell's Essay on the Poets of Renfrewshire (p. xvii.) prefixed to the Harp of Renfrewshire. Paisley, 1819, 12mo.

[2] Wood's Peerage of Scotland, vol. ii. p. 494.

Dempster, the poet died in 1595 ;[1] but the peer is known to have survived till 1611. Whatever credit may be due to this literary historian, there are other circumstances more than sufficient to render their identity extremely dubious. Montgomery, in a sonnet addressed to Robert Hudson, specifies Semple as not exempted from the ordinary misfortunes of poets ; and as this sonnet appears to have been written when he was advanced in years, it affords another presumption against the identity of the poet and the peer.

> Ye knau ill guyding genders mony gees,
> And specially in poets : for example,
> Ye can pen out tua cuple, and ye pleis,
> Yourself and I, old Scot and Robert Semple.[2]

It is not perhaps to be considered as very probable that Montgomery would have applied these expressions to the presumptive heir of a baron ; and it is certain that he would not thus have described the baron himself. There is some reason to believe that Semple was a captain in the army : he speaks of himself as having been present at the siege of Edinburgh Castle ; in the progress of his narrative, he specifies particular incidents which he had not himself

---

[1] Dempsteri Historia Ecclesiastica Gentis Scotorum, p. 602.—He represents Semple as exhibiting the combined excellencies of Propertius, Tibullus, Ovid, and Callimachus ; an eulogium which cannot but be regarded as extravagant by those who have perused such of his compositions as are now to be found.

[2] Montgomery's Poems, p. 75. Edinb. 1821, 8vo.

an opportunity of observing, and he distinctly mentions a captain of his own name.

> Four capitanis followit, at thair bak to byde,
> Sempill and Hectour, Ramsay and Robesoun.

The comedy of Philotus exhibits a plot sufficiently complex. The principal character, from which the play derives its name, is a very rich and very old man, deeply enamoured of Emily, the young and beautiful daughter of Alberto. As she feels little inclination to listen to the addresses of such a lover, he employs a *macrell*, or procuress, " to allure the madyn ;" though, with his honourable intentions, it is not very obvious why he should have had recourse to an agent of this class. In the course of a long conference, she endeavours, but without success, to persuade Emily to marry Philotus. Some of her suggestions may be supposed to reflect considerable light on the usages of that period. He afterwards addresses himself to Alberto, who very willingly listens to his proposal, and endeavours to obtain his daughter's consent ; but she declares her repugnance to such a match, and thus excites the violent indignation of her father. Flavius, a youthful lover, now makes his appearance, and finds a more favourable reception. He commences with a long and pedantic oration, interspersed with divers notices of Apollo, Daphne, Mars, Venus, Demosthenes, and other notable personages. We may suppose the young gentleman to be newly dismissed from the schools, but the young gentlewoman seems to be equally familiar with Parnassus and Helicon.

> Last, sen ze may my meladie remeid,
>> Releiue zour Sysiphus of his restles stane :
> Zour Titius breist that dois full ryfely bleid,
>> Grant grace thairto, befoir the grip be gane.
> Cum stanche the thrist of Tantalus anone,
> And cure the wounds geuin with Achilles knyfe :[1]
>> Accept for zours, fair maistres, such a one,
> That for zour saik dar sacrifice his lyfe.

[1] Telephus, when wounded by Achilles, could only be cured by the spear which had inflicted the injury. See Hygini Fabulae, p. 161, edit. Munckeri, and Musgrave's Euripides, vol. iii. p. 588. This subject has furnished the ancient poets with many allusions, which are frequently of the amatory kind. The following distich Valckenaer has quoted from a manuscript Anthology. (Diatribe in Euripidis perditorum Dramatum Reliquias, p. 210. Lugd. Bat. 1767, 4to.)

> Τήλεφον ὁ τρώσας καὶ ἀκέσσατο· μὴ σύγε κούρη
> Εἰς ἐμὲ δυσμενίων γίνεο πικροτέρη.

The entire story is contained in an epigram of another ancient poet. (Poematia vetera Pithoei, p. 49. Anthologia Burmanni, tom. i. p. 80.)

> Telephus excellens Alcidis pignus et Augae
>> Externae sortis bella inopina tulit.
> Nam Grai Trojam peterent cum mille carinis,
>> Tangeret et classis litus adacta suum,
> Occurrens Danais forti dum pugnat Achilli,
>> Syria pugnanti percutit hasta femur.
> Pro cujus cura consultus dixit Apollo,
>> Hostica quod salubrem cuspis haberet opem.

EMILY. Zour orisoun, sir, sounds with sic skil,
  In Cupids court as ze had bene vpbrocht,
Or fosterit in Parnassus forkit hill,
  Quhair poetis hes thair flame and furie socht,
  Nocht taisting of sweit Helicon for nocht,
As be zour plesant preface dois appeir,
  Tending thairby, quhill as we haue na thocht,
To mak vs to zour purpois to adheir.

Emily assumes the dress of a young gentleman, and in this disguise leaves her father's house. In the mean time, her brother Philerno returning after a long absence, is mistaken for Emily, to whom he bears a striking resemblance: he concurs in his sister's stratagem, and consents to marry Philotus; who commits his supposed bride to the custody of Brisilla, his daughter by a former marriage. This youthful pair find themselves pleased with each other's company; and, after certain invocations, Philerno pretends to be metamorphosed into a man. An interval of a month is supposed to elapse between the elopement of Emily and the nuptials of Philo-

Mox precibus flexi Pelidae robore sacro
Injecto membris pulvere plaga fuit.
Monstrant fata viri vario miracula casu :
Unde datum est vulnus, contigit inde salus.

In the eighth of these verses, the poet has shortened the penult of *salubrem ;* and several modern poets have ventured to follow the example. Among this number is Buchanan, Psalm, xcix, whose error was long ago noted by Pincier. (Parerga Otii Marpurgensis Philologica, p. 380. Herbornæ Nassov. 1617, 8vo.)

tus; but the period at length arrives, and a priest performs the marriage-ceremony with sufficient formality. Philerno, " fearing to be discovered, maketh a brawling that same night with Philotus, and abuseth him vyllie, and to colour the mater the better, agreeth with a whore to go to bed with Philotus." Flavius, who had been secretly married to Emily, is struck with astonishment on witnessing the marriage of this old man to a person whom he supposes to be the real daughter of Alberto; and, after various conjurations, he dismisses her as an evil spirit who had assumed an earthly shape. She returns to her father's house, and is there met by Philotus: the one complains of her husband, and the other of his wife, and a comic situation is thus produced. The mystery being at length explained, Emily returns to Flavius, and Brisilla is married to Philerno. After this arrangement of their domestic affairs, Philotus expatiates on his own folly, and a person named the Messenger makes a concluding address to the audience.

This comedy, in its plan and execution, discovers a much nearer approach to the modern drama than Sir David Lindsay's " Satyre of the three Estaitis." It possesses the merit of easy versification, but the speeches are frequently too long and declamatory. The author has not divided his play into acts and scenes. The probability of the incidents is sometimes impaired by the introduction of a certain character denominated the Pleasant, who, without any apparent concern in the business of the drama, intrudes himself into the most private conferences for the mere purpose of aiming at a joke.

The plot and indeed the entire story of Philotus are borrowed from a work of Barnaby Rich, published under the title of " Rich his Farewell to Militarie Profession ; conteining very pleasant Discourses fit for a peaceable time." The work includes eight different tales, of which he has given this preliminary account : " The histories (altogether) are eight in number, whereof the first, the seconde, the fift, the seuenth, and eight are tales that are but forged onely for delight, neither credible to be beleued, nor hurt- full to be perused. The third, the fowerth, and the sixt are Italian histories, written likewise for pleasure, by Maister L. B." The tale of Phylotus and Emelia is the eighth in the series, and, according to this account, belongs to the author's original stock. As the book is of great rarity, it has been thought advisable to in- sert this tale in an appendix. For the use of a mutilated copy of a very early, if not the first edition, we are indebted to Charles Kirkpatrick Sharpe, Esq. It is a small quarto, printed in black letter ; but as it wants the title and nearly all the last leaf, the date cannot be ascertained. The first edition is said to have been printed in the year 1583. In the following reprint of the eighth tale, the defects of this copy have, by the kindness of Dr Bliss, been supplied from the edition of 1606, a copy of which is preserved in the Bodleian Library at Oxford. The passages taken from the latter impression are distinguished by being enclosed in brackets. Rich's second tale, of Apolonius and Silla, appears to have furnished the plot of Shakspeare's Twelfth Night.[1]

In what he entitles the Conclusion, he has introduced a tale of a certain devil named Balthaser, who married a young lady of singular beauty, rejoicing in the name of Mildred. The husband was so pestered with the wife's love of the new fashions in dress, that he finally determined to relinquish the connexion; and, in pursuance of this resolution, he directed his course to Edinburgh, where he possessed the king of Scots. "While Mistres Mildred was proceeding in these speeches or suche other like, the deuill her housbande was stroke in suche a dumpe, that not able any longer to indure her talke, he not onely auoided hymself from her presence, but also deuised with speede to flie the countrie, and cummyng to Douer, thinkyng to crosse the seas, finding no shippyng readie, he altered his course, and gat hym into Scotlande, neuer staiyng till he came to Edenbrough, where the kyng kept his court; and now forgettyng all humanitie whiche he had learned before in Englande, he began againe a freshe to plaie the deuil, and so possessed the king of Scots himself with such strange and vnaquainted passions, that by the coniecture of phisitions, and other learned men that were then assembled together, to iudge the kynges diseases,

---

[1] See Boswell's Shakspeare, vol. xi. p. 321. Collier's Annals of the Stage, vol. i. p. 328, and likewise his Poetical Decameron, vol. ii. p. 134.

thei all concluded that it must needes bee some feende of hell that so disturbde their prince." Such is the story as it stands in the earlier edition ; but before the year 1606, a king of Scots had become formidable to an English author or printer, and in the later edition we find a prudent substitution of the Grand Turk. " Thinking to crosse the seas, finding shipping ready, he toke his course and gat him to Rome, neuer staiyng till he came to Constantinople, where the Turke kept his court ; and nowe forgetting all humanitie which he had learned before in England, he began againe afresh to play the deuill, and so possessed the Turke himselfe."

The comedy of Philotus is here reprinted from a copy of the first edition deposited in the Advocates' Library. A second edition of this delectable treatise was printed at Edinburgh by Andrew Hart in the year 1612. Both editions are in quarto, and both are extremely rare. The song inserted at the end of the first edition, and omitted in the second, is transcribed from Campion ; and, according to the opinion of Mr Crowe, it exhibits " the most extraordinary combination of English verse that is perhaps any where to be found." [1] From a copy belonging to the Duke of Devonshire, the various readings of the second edition have been very politely supplied by J. Payne Collier, Esq. It has not been considered of any importance to mark such variations as are merely

[1] Crowe's Treatise on English Versification, p. 105. Lond. 1827, 8vo.

literal. Here we clearly perceive such corrections and changes as may be supposed to have proceeded from the author; nor is it necessary to discuss the hasty conclusion of Mr Pinkerton, which he himself deliberately abandoned, that Philotus must have been written long before the date of the first impression, that it must have been written during the reign of James the Fifth.

The indecency of this early drama rendered it a matter of no small doubt and hesitation, whether we could venture to reprint it without suppressing the most flagrant passages; of which we do not feel inclined to adopt the defence urged by a learned writer, to whom we have already referred. " The recent editor of a *Biographia Dramatica*," he states, " has attacked this piece violently on the score of immodesty. This writer's philosophy, it would seem, is exactly equal to his learning. Had he the smallest share of philosophy, he would know that our bashfulness, so remarkable to foreigners, is a weakness, and not a virtue; and that it is this bashfulness alone which makes us so nice about matters so freely discoursed by other nations. If the generation of man be a matter of shame and infamy, it follows that man is the child of shame and infamy. Now nothing excites vice so much as low ideas of human nature; and those nice writers, while they are preaching virtue, are from mere ignorance opening the door to every vice. Had this writer any learning, he would know that the comedies of Aristophanes, written in the brightest period of

Athenian politeness, are quite indecent to British ears. Are we wiser than the Athenians? Are we not far more foolish in this respect than all modern nations?" [1] Of the validity of this extraordinary defence he seems however to have felt a secret distrust, or perhaps his abstract science was encountered by the bookseller's homely prejudice; for, after an interval of six years, when he republished the same comedy,[2] he suppressed those very passages which he here represents as so consonant to the dictates of sound philosophy, as well as Attic taste. Without entertaining the faintest wish to study moral science under so great a master, we have been induced to hope that the peculiar circumstances of such a reprint as this, overshadowed by the decent veil of Gothic characters, and confined to a narrow and select circulation, might be considered as affording some justification of our departure from the plan of a family Philotus.

---

[1] Pinkerton's List of the Scotish Poets, (p. cxi.) prefixed to Ancient Scotish Poems. Lond. 1786, 2 vols. 8vo.

[2] Scotish Poems, reprinted from scarce editions, vol. iii. p. 1. Lond. 1792, 3 vols. 8vo.

Ane verie excellent and delecta- bill Treatiſe intitulit

PHILOTVS.

QVHAIRIN WE MAY PERSAVE THE

greit inconveniences that fallis out in the

Mariage betvvene age and zouth.

Ovid.

Siqua velis aptè nubere,nube pari.

IMPRINTED AT EDINBVRGH

be Robert Charteris.　1603.

CVM PRIVILEGIO REGALI.

THE NAMES OF THE INTER-
LOQVITORS.

Ane verie excellent and delecta-
bill Treatise intitulit

PHILOTVS.

Philotus directis his speich to Emilie.

Lustie luiffome lamp of licht,
Zour bonynes zour bewtie bricht
Zour staitly stature trym & ticht
    With gesture graue and gude:
Zour countenance, zour cullour
Zour lauching lips, zour smyling cheir,   (cleir
Zour properties dois all appear,
    My senses to illude.

2 Quhen I zour bewtie do behald,
I man vnto zour fairnes fald:
I dow not flie howbeit I wald,
    Bot bound I man be zouris:
For zow sweit hart I wald forsaik,
The Empyre for to be my maik,
Thairfoir deir dow sum pitie tak,
    And saif mee fra the schowres.

3 Deme na ill of my age my dow,
Ise play the zonkeris part to zow.
First try the treuth, then may ze trow,
    Gif I mynd to desaue:
For Gold nor geir ze sall not want,
Sweit hart with me thairs be na scant,
Thairfoir some grace vntome grant,
    For courtesie I craue.

He wantis na jewels claith nor waith,
    Bot is baith big and beine.

12 Weill war the woman all hir lyfe,
Had hap to be his weddit wyfe,
Scho micht haue gold and geir als ryfe,
    As Copper in hir kist:
Zea, not a Ladie in all this Land,
I wait micht haue mair wealth in hand,
Nor micht haue mair at hir command,
    To do with quhat scho list.

13 Fair floure, now sen ze may him fang,
It war not gude to let him gang,
Unto zour self ze'ile do greit wrang,
    Sweit hart now and ze slip him:
Now thair is twentie into this toun,
Of greitest riches and renoun,
That wald be glad for to sit doun,
    Upon thair kneis to grip him.

14 Thocht he be auld my joy, quhat reck,
Quhen he is gane giue him ane geck,
And tak another be the neck,
    Quhen ze the graith haue gottin:
Schaw me zour mynd and quhat ze meine,
I sall conuoy all this sa cleine,
That me ze fall esteime ane freine,
    Quhen I am deid and rottin.

15 Emilie. I grant gude-wyfe he is richt gude,
Ane man of wealth and nobill blude,
Bot hes mair mister of ane Hude,
    And Mittanes till his handis:
Nor of ane bairnelie Lasse lyke mee,
Mair meit his Oy nor wyfe to be:

                                    His

His age and myne cannot agrie,
    Quhill that the warld standis.

16 Macrell. Let that allane, he is not sa auld,
Nor zit of curage half sa cald,
Bot gif ze war his wypfe, ze wald,
    Be weill aneuch content.
With him mair treitment on ane day,
And get mair making off ze may,
Nor with ane Wamfler, suith to say,
    Quhen twentie zeiris ar spent.

17 Ze neyther mell with lad nor loun,
Bot with the best in all this toun,
His wyfe may ay sit formest doun,
    At eyther burde or bink:
Gang formest in at dure or zet,
And ay the first gude-day wald get,
With all men honourit and weill tzet,
    As onie hart wald think.

18 Se quhat a womans mynde may meise
And heir quhat honour, wealth and eise,
Ze may get with him and ze pleise,
    To do as I deuyse:
Zour fyre sall first be birnand cleir,
Zour Madynis than sall haue zour geir,
Put in gude ordour and effeir,
    Ilk morning or zow ryse.

19 And say, lo Maistres heir zour Muillis,
Put on zour Uplicote for it cuillis,
Lo, heir ane of zour Ueluote stuillis,
    Quhairon ze sall sit doun:
Than twasum cummis to cambe zour hair,
Put on your heidgeir soft and fair,

B

Plesant. Ha, ha, quha brocht thir kittocks hither
The mekill feind resaue the sithir:
I trow ʒe was not al together,
    This twel-month at ane preiching.
Allace I lauch for lytill lucke,
I lauch to sie ane auld Carle gucke:
Wow wow sa faine as he wald k ,
    Fra he fall till his sleitching.

5 Now wallie as the Carle he caiges,
Gudeman quha hes maid ʒour mustages?
Lo as the boy of fourescoir ages,
    As he micht not be biddin:
Came ʒe to wow our Lasse, now lachter,
ʒe ar sa rasch thair will be slachter,
ʒe will not spair nor speir quhais aucht hir,
    ʒe ar sa raschlie riddin.

6 Emily. I wait not weill sir quhat ʒe meine,
Bot suirlie I haue seindill seine,
Ane wower of ʒour ʒeiris sa keine,
    As ʒe appeir to be:
I think ane man sir, of ʒour ʒeiris,
Sould not be blyndit with the bleiris,
Ga seik ane partie of ʒour peires,
    For ʒe get nane of mee.

The auld man speikis to the Macrell to allure the Madyn.

7 Gude Dame, I haue ʒow to imploy,
Sa ʒe my purpose can convoy:
And that ʒon Lasse I micht inioy,
    ʒe sould not want rewaird:
Giue hir this Tablet and this Ring,
This Pursse of gold and spair nathing:
Sa ʒe about all weill may bring,
              Of gold

Of gold tak na regaird.

8. Macrell. Na fir, let me and that allane,
Suppofe fcho war maid of a ftane,
Ife gar hir grant oz all be gane,
　　To be at zour command:
Thocht fcho be ftrange, I think na wonder,
Blait things is fone bzocht in ane blunder,
Scho is not the firft fir, of ane hunder,
　　That I haue had in hand.

9 I am ane Fifche I am ane Eile,
Can fteir my toung and tayle richt weill,
I giue me to the mekill Deill,
　　Gif onie can do mair:
I can with fair anis fleitch and flatter,
And win ane Crown bot with ane clatter,
That gars me dzink gude wyne foz watter,
　　Suppois my back ga bair.

　　The Macrell intends to allure the Madyn.

10 God blis zow Maiftres with zour Buik,
Leife me thay lips that I on luik:
I hope in God to fie zow bzuik,
　　Ane nobill houfe at hame:
I ken ane Man into this toun,
Of hyeft honour and renoun,
That wald be glaid to giue his Gowne,
　　Foz to haue zow his Dame.

11 Emily. Now be my faull I can not fie,
That thair fik vertew is in me,
Gudwyfe, I pray zow quhat is he,
　　That man quhome of ze meine?
Macrell. Philotus is the man a faith,
Ane ground-riche man and full of graith:

He wantis na jewels claith nor waith,
   Bot is baith big and beine.

12 Weill war the woman all hir lyfe,
Had hap to be his weddit wyfe,
Scho micht haue gold and geir als ryfe,
   As Copper in hir kift:
Zea, not a Ladie in all this Land,
I wait micht haue mair wealth in hand,
Nor micht haue mair at hir command,
   To do with quhat scho lift.

13 Fair floure, now sen ze may him fang,
It war not gude to let him gang,
Unto zour self ze'ile do greit wrang,
   Sweit hart now and ze flip him:
Now thair is twentie into this toun,
Of greitest riches and renoun,
That wald be glad for to sit doun,
   Upon thair kneis to grip him.

14 Thocht he be auld my joy, quhat reck,
Quhen he is gane giue him ane geck,
And tak another be the neck,
   Quhen ze the graith haue gottin:
Schaw me zour mynd and quhat ze meine,
I sall conuoy all this sa cleine,
That me zee sall esteme ane freine,
   Quhen I am deid and rottin.

15 Emilie. I grant gude-wyfe he is richt gude,
Ane man of wealth and nobill blude,
Bot hes mair mister of ane Hude,
   And Mittanes till his handis:
Nor of ane bairnelie Lasse lyke mee,
Mair meit his Oy nor wyfe to be:

                             His

His age and myne cannot agrie,
    Quhill that the warld standis.

16 Macrell. Let that allane, he is not sa auld,
Nor zit of curage half sa cald,
Bot gif ze war his wyfe, ze wald,
    Be weill aneuch content.
With him mair treitment on ane day,
And get mair making off ze may,
Nor with ane Wamster, suith to say,
    Quhen twentie zeiris ar spent.

17 Ze neyther mell with lad nor loun,
Bot with the best in all this toun,
His wyfe may ay sit formest doun,
    At eyther burde or bink:
Gang formest in at dure or zet,
And ay the first gude-day wald get,
With all men honourit and weill tzet,
    As onie hart wald think.

18 Se quhat a womans mynde may meise
And heir quhat honour, wealth and eise,
Ze may get with him and ze pleise,
    To do as I deuyse:
Zour fyre sall first be birnand cleir,
Zour Madynis than sall haue zour geir,
Put in gude ordour and effeir,
    Ilk morning or zow ryse.

19 And say, lo Maistres heir zour Muillis,
Put on zour Wylicote for it cuillis,
Lo, heir ane of zour Ueluote stuillis,
    Quhairon ze sall sit doun:
Than twasum cummis to cambe zour hair,
Put on your heidgeir soft and fair,

B

Tak thair zour glasse sie all be clair,
And sa gais on zour Goun.

20 Than tak to stanche the morning drouth,
Ane cup of Mauesie for zour mouth,
For sume cast sucker in at fouth,
    Togidder with a Toist:
Thrie Garden gowps tak of the Air,
And bid zour Page in haist prepair,
For zour Disione sum daintie fair,
    And cair not for na coist.

21 Ane pair of Pleuaris pypping hait,
Ane Pertrick and ane Quailzie get,
Ane cup of Sack, sweit and weill set,
    May for ane breckfast gaine.
Zour Cater he may cair for syne,
Sum delicate agane ze dyne,
Zour Cuke to seasoun all sa fyne,
    Than dois imploy his paine.

22 To sie zour seruantes may ze gang,
And luke zour Madynis all amang,
And gif thair onie wark be wrang,
    Than bitterlie them blame.
Than may ze haue baith Quaiffis and Kellis,
Hich Candie Ruffes and Barlet Bellis,
All for zour weiring and not ellis,
    Maid in zour hous at hame.

23 And now quhen all thir warks is done,
For zour refresching efternone,
Gar bring vnto zour chalmer sone,
    Sum daintie dische of meate:
Ane cup or twa with Muscadall,
Sum vther licht thing thairwithall,

For

For Rasins or for Capers call,
 Gif that ze pleaſe to eate.

24 Till ſupper tyme then may ze chois,
Unto zour Garden to repois,
Or merelie to tak ane glois,
 Or tak ane buke and reid on:
Syne to zour ſupper ar ze brocht,
Till fair full far that hes bene focht,
And daintie diſches deirlie bocht,
 That Ladies loues to feid on.

25 The Organes than into zour hall,
With Schalme and Cymbrell ſound thay ſall,
The Upole and the Lute with all,
 To gar zour meate diſgeſt:
The ſupper done than vp ze ryſe,
To gang ane quhyle as is the gyſe,
Be ze haue rowmit ane Alley thryſe,
 It is ane myle almaiſt.

26 Than may ze to zour Chalmer gang,
Begyle the nicht gif it be lang,
With talk and merie mowes amang,
 To eleuate the ſplene:
For zour Collation tak and taiſt,
Sum lytill licht thing till diſgeſt,
At nicht vſe Renſe wyne ay almaiſt,
 For it is cauld and clene.

27 And for zour back I dar be bould,
That ze ſall weir euen as ze would,
With doubill Garniſchings of gould,
 And Craip aboue zour hair:
Zour Ueluote hat, zour Hude of Stait,
Zour Myſſell quhen ze gang to gait,

Fra Sone and wind baith air and lait,
    To keip that face sa fair.

28 Of Pareis wark wrocht by the laif,
Zour fyne Half-cheinzeis ze sall haue,
For to decoir ane Carkat craif
    That cumlie Collour bane:
Zour greit gould Cheinzie for zour neck,
Be bowsum to the Carle and beck,
For he hes gould aneuch, quhat reck?
    It will not stand on nane.

29 And for zour Gownes ay the new guyse,
Ze with zour Tailzeours may deuyse,
To haue them louse with plets and plyis,
    Or clasped clois behind:
The stuffe my hart ze neid not haine,
Pan Ueluot, raysde figurit or plaine,
Silk, Satyne, Damayse or Grograine,
    The fynest ze can find.

30 Zour claithes on cullouris cuttit out,
And all Pasmentit round about,
My blessing on that semelie snout,
    Sa weill I trow sall set them:
Zour schankis of silk zour veluot schone,
Zour borderit Wylicote abone,
As ze deuyse all sall be done,
    Uncraisit quhen ze get them.

31 Zour Tablet be zour hals that hinges
Gould bracelets and all vther things,
And all zour fingers full of Rings,
    With Pearle and precious stanes:
Ze sall haue ay quhill ze cry ho,
Rickillis of gould and jewellis io,

                Quhat

Quhat reck to tak the Bogill-bo,
   My bonie burd for anis.

32 Sweit hart quhat farther wald ye haue:
Quhat greiter plesour wald ʒe craue,
Now be my saull ʒow will desaue,
   ʒour self and ʒe forsaik him:
Thairfoir sweit honie I ʒow pray,
Tak tent in tyme and nocht delay,
Sweit sucker, neck me not with nay,
   Bot be content to tak him.

33 Plesant. The deuill cum lick that beird auld
Now sie the trottibus and trowane,   (rowan
Sa busilie as sho is wowane,
   Sie as the carling craks:
Begyle the barne sho is bot ʒoung,
Foull fall thay lips, God nor that toung,
War doubill gilt with Murisch doung,
   And ill cheir on thay cheikis.

34 Emily. Gude-wyfe all is bot gude I heir,
For weill I lufe to mak gude cheir,
For honouris, gould, and vther geir,
   Thay can not be refusit:
I grant indeid, my daylie fair,
Will be sufficient and mair,
Bot be it gude ʒe do not spair,
   As royallie to ruse it.

35 I grant all day to be weill tret,
Honours anew and hicht vpset,
Bot quhat intreatment sall I get,
   I pray ʒow in my bed?
Bot with ane lairbair for to ly,
Ane auld deid stock, baith cauld and dry,

And all my dayes heir I deny,
    That he my schankes sched.

36 His eine half sunkin in his heid,
His Lyre far caulder than the leid,
His frostie flesch as he war deid,
    Will for na happing heit:
Unhealthsum hosting euer mair,
His filthsum flewme is nathing fair,
Ay rumisching with rift and rair,
    Now, wow gif that be sweit,

37. His skynne hard clappit to the bane,
With Gut and Grauell baith ouirgane,
Now quhen thir troubles hes him tane,
    His wyfe gets all the wyte:
For Uenus games I let them ga,
I gesse hee be not gude of thay,
I could weill of his maners ma,
    Gif I list till indyte.

38 Macrell. For Uenus game care not a cuit,
Waill me ane Wamsler that can do'it,
Sen thair may be na vther buit,
    Plat on his head ane horne:
Handill me that with wit and skill,
Ze may haue easments at zour will,
At nicht gar zoung men cum zow till,
    Put them away at morne.

39 Emily. Gude-wyfe, all is bot vaine ze seik,
To mee of sik maters to speik,
Zour purpois is not worth ane leik,
    I will heir zow na mair:
Mark Dame, and this is all and sum,
If euer ze this earand cum,

Dʒ of ʒour head I heir ane mum,
    Ʒe fall repent it fair.

40 Macrell. Ʒon daintie Dame fcho is fa nyce
Sche'ill nocht be win be na deupce,
Foʒ nouther pʒayer noʒ foʒ pʒyce,
    Foʒ gould noʒ vther gaine.
Scho is fa ackwart and fa thʒa,
That with refufe I come hir fra,
Scho, be Sanct Marie faynde mee fa,
    I dar not ga agane.

Philotus enteris in conference with the Madynis father.

41. Gude Goffe, fen ʒe haue euer bene,
My trew and auld familiar freind,
To mak mair quentance vs betwene,
    I glaidly could agrie:
Ʒe haue ane douchter quhome vntill,
I beare ane paffing grit gude will,
Quhais Phifnomie pʒefigures skill,
    With wit and honeffie.

42 Gif mee that Laffe to be my wyfe,
Foʒ Tocher-gude fall be na ftryfe,
Beleiue mee fcho fall haue ane lyfe,
    And foʒ ʒour geir I cair not:
Faith ʒe ʒour felf fall modifie,
Hir Lyfe Rent Land and Conjunctfie,
And Goffop, quhair thay fame fall be,
    Appoynt the place and fpair not.

43 Betwixt vs twa the Hepʒis-maill,
Sall bʒuik my heritage all haill,
Quhilks gif that thay happen to faill,
    To her Hepʒis quhat faeuer:
My moueables I will deuyde,

Ane pairt my Douchter to prouyde,
Ane pairt to leaue sum freind asyde,
　　Quhen deith sall vs disseuer.

44 Alberto. Gude sir, and gossop I am glaid,
That all be done as ze haue said,
Tak baith my blissing and the Mayd,
　　Hame to zour hous togidder:
And gif that scho play not hir pairt,
In onie lawfull honest airt,
And honour zow with all hir hairt,
　　I wald scho gaid not thither.

　　　Alberto speiks to his Dochter.

45 For the ane man I haue foreseine,
Ane man of micht and welth I meine,
That staitlier may the susteine,
　　Nor ony of all thy kin:
Ane man of honour and renoun,
Ane of the Potentes of the toun:
Quhair nane may beinlier sit doun,
　　This Citie all within.

46 Emily. God and gude nature dois allow,
That I obedient be to zow,
And father hithertils I trow,
　　Ze haue nane vther seine:
And als estemis zow for to be,
Ane louing father vnto mee,
Thairfoir deir father let mee see,
　　The man of quhome ze meine.

47 Alberto. Philotus is the man indeid,
Quhair thow ane nobill lyfe may leid,
With quhom I did sa far proceid,
　　Wee want bot thy gude will:

　　　　　　　　　　　　Now

Now giue thy frie consent thairfoir,
Deck vp and do thyself decoir,
Gang quicklie to and say no moir,
    Thow man agrie thairtill.

48 Emilie. Gif ʒe fra furie wald refraine,
And patientlie heir me agane,
I sould ʒow schaw in termis plane,
    With reason ane excuse:
Sen Mariage bene but thraldome free,
God and gude nature dois agree,
That I quhair as it lykes not mee,
    May lawfullie refuse.

49 I am fourtene,and hee fourescoir,
I haill and sound,hee seik and soir,
How can I giue consent thairfoir,
    Oꝛ ʒit till him agree?
Judge gif Philotus be discreit,
To seik ane match sa far vnmeit,
Thocht I rufuse him father sweit,
    I pꝛay ʒow pardon mee.

50 Alberto. How durst thow trumper be sa
To tant oꝛ tell,that he was ald?   (bald
Oꝛ durst refuse ocht that I wald,
    Haue biddin the obey:
Bot sen ʒe stand sa lytill aw,
Ise gar ʒow Maistres foꝛ to knaw,
The Impyꝛe Parents hes be law,
    Abuif thair Childꝛen ay.

51 And heir to God I mak ane vow,
Bot gif thow at my bidding bow,
I sall the dꝛesse and harkin how,
    And syne aduyse the better:
      C

I sall thee cast intill ane pit,
Quhair thow for zeir and day sall sit,
With breid and water surely knit
    Hard bound intill ane fetter.

52 Thow sat sa soft vpon thy stuill,
That making off maid the ane fuill,
Bot I sall mak thy curage cuill,
    For all thy stomack stout:
That efterwards quhill that thow leif,
Thou's be agast mee for to greif.
Perchance thow greines that play to preif,
    Aduyse thee and speik out.

53 Emily. Sweit father, mitigate zour rage,
Zour wraith and anger sir, aswage,
Haue pitie on my zouthlie age,
    Zour awin flesch and zour blude:
Gif in your pre I be outthrawin,
Quhome haue ze wraikit bot zour awin,
Sic crweltie hes not bene knawin,
    Amang the Turckes sa rude.

54 The sauage beists into thair kynde,
Thair zoung to pitie ar inclynde,
Let mercie thairfoir muif your mynde,
    To her that humblie cryis:
Tak vp and lenifie zour yre,
Suspend the furie of zour fyre,
And grant me layser, I desyre,
    Ane lytill to aduyse.

Heir followis the Oratioun of the zonker Flavius to the
Madyn, hir anſwer and conſent, The convoying of her from
her father: her father and the auld wower followis, and finds
Philerno the Madyns brother laitlie arryued, quhome they
tak to be the Madyn, and of his deceit.

                                         The

The raging low, the feirce and flaming fyre
That dois my breiſt and body al combure
Incendit with the dart of grit deſyre,
Fra force of theſe twa ſparking eyis ful ſure,
Hes me conſtraynit to cum and ſeik my cure
Of her,fra quhom proceidit hes my wound,
Quhom neyther Salue nor Syrop can aſſure,
Bot only ſho can mak me ſaif and ſound.

56 Lyke as the captiue with ane tyrant taine,
Perforce with promiſe toiſtit to and fro,
Quhen that he ſeis all vther graces gaine,
Man ſuccour ſeik of him that wrocht his wo,
Sa mon I fald to my maiſt freindly fo,
To ſeik for ſalue of her that gaue the ſair:
To pray for peace,thocht rigour bid me go,
To cry for mercie,quhen as I may na mair.

57 Sa ſen ʒe haue me captiuate as thrall,
Sen ʒe preuaill,let pitie now haue place:
Haue mercie ſen ʒe Maiſtres ar of all,
Grudge not to grant ʒour ſupplicant ſum grace
To ſlay ane taine man,war bot lack allace,
Fra that he cum voluntarlie in will:
Sen I am,Miſtres,in the ſelf ſame cace,
Ane thrall conſenting pitie war to ſpill.

58 Quhat ferly thocht,puir I with luif oppreſt
Confes the force of the blynd Archer Boye
How was Appollo for his Daphne dreſt,
And Mars amaſit his Uenus to enjoy,
Did not the thundering Jupiter convoy
For Danae him ſelf into ane ſhowre,
The gods aboue ſen luif hath maid them coy,
Unto his law then quhy ſould I not lowre?

C 2

59 As taine with ane nor Daphne mair decoir
Quhais vult to Uenus may compairit be:
And bene in bewtie Danae befoir.
Suppose the God on hir did cast his eye:
Quhais graces to hir bewtie dois agrie,
And in quhais fairnes is no foly found,
Quhat meruell Mistres than, suppose ze se,
With willing band me to zour bewtie bound.

60 Quhais bricht contepning bewtie with the
Na les al vther pulchritude dois pas (beamis
Nor to compair ane clud w͏ glansing gleames,
Bricht Uenus cullour with ane landwart las:
The quhytest layke bot with the blackest asse,
The rubent Rois bot with the wallowit weid
As purest gold is preciouser nor glasse,
Zour bewtie sa all vtherdois exceid.

61 Zour hair lyk gold, & lyke the Pole zour eye
Zour snawisch cheiks lyke quhytest Allabast,
Zour louesum lips sad, soft, and sweit wee sie,
As Roses red quhen that ane showre is past:
Zour toung micht mak Demosthenes agast,
Zour teith ye peirls micht of thair place depryue
With Bwillis of Indian Ebur at the last
Zour Papis for the priozitie dois stryue.

62 And lyke as quhen the stamping seale is set
In war weill wrocht, quhill it is soft I say,
The prent thairof remayning may ze get,
Suppois the seale itself be tane away,
Zour semlie shaip sa sall abyde for ay,
Quhilk throw the sicht my sensis hes ressaisit,
Thocht absent ze, zit I sall nicht and day,
Zour presence haue as in my hart ingraisit.

63 Thocht

63 Thocht fansie be bot of ane figure fainit,
Na figure feids quhair thair is na effect:
Euin fa fweit faull I perifch bot as painit,
With fansie fed that will na fafting breck,
Suppois I haue the accident quhat reck,
Grant me the folide fubftance to atteine,
Gif not,quhen ʒe to deith fall me direct,
Quhom bot ʒour awin haue ʒe côfoundit clein?

64 Laft,fen ʒe may my meladie remeid,
Releiue ʒour Syfiphus of his reftles ftane:
ʒour Citius breift that dois full ryfely bleid,
Grant grace thairto,befoir the grip be gane,
Cum ftanche the thrift of Cantalus anone,
And cure ye wounds geuin with Achilles knyfe
Accept for ʒours fair Maiftres,fuch a one,
That for ʒour faik dar facrifice his lyfe.

65 Emily. ZOVR Difcoun fir founds with fic fkil
In Cupids Court as ʒe had bene vpbrocht:
Or fofterit in Parnaffus forkit Hill
Quhair Poetis hes thair flame and furie focht
Nocht taifting of fweit Helicon for nocht,
As be ʒour plefant preface dois appeir:
Tending thairby,quhill as we haue na thocht,
To mak vs to ʒour purpois to adheir.

66 With louing language tending till allure,
With fweit difcourfe the fimpill till outrfyle,
ʒe caft ʒour craft,ʒour cunning and ʒour cure,
Bot puir Orphanes and Madynis to begyle,
ʒour waillit out words,inventit for a wyle,
To trap all thofe that trowis in ʒow na traine
The frute of flattrie is bot to defyle,
And fpred that wee can neuer get agane.

C 3

67 ʒe gar vs trow that all our heids be cowtt,
In praysing of our bewtie by the Skyis:
Quht in ʒour wordds we ar na mair bot mowtt
This way to sie gif vs ʒe may supprʒyse,
ʒour doubill hart dois euerie day deuyse,
Ane thowsand shifts was neuer in ʒour thocht,
ʒe labour thus with all that in ʒow lyis,
For till vndo, and bring vs all to nocht.

68 And this conceate is common to ʒow all,
For ʒour awin lust, ʒe set not by our schame,
ʒour sweitest word, ar seasonit all with gall,
ʒour fairest phrase, disfigures bot defame,
I think thairfoir thay gritlie ar to blame,
That trowis in ʒow mair nor the thing thay se
Bot I, quhill that Emilia is my Name
To trow I sall like to Sanct Thomas be.

69 Flavius. For feir sweit maistres quhat remeid
Quha may perswade quhair thair is dreid:
ʒit deme ʒe wrangouslie in deid,
        Now be my saull I sweir:
ʒour honour, not ʒour schame I seik,
I count not by my lust ane leik,
It was na sik thing Maistres meik,
        That maid me to cum heir.

70 This is my sute ʒe sall me trust,
Judge ʒe ʒour self gif it be just,
In honest luif and honest lust,
        With ʒow to leid my lyfe:
This is the treuth of my intent,
In lawfull lufe bot onlie bent,
Aduyse ʒow gif ʒe can consent,
        To be my weddit wyfe.

                                    71 Emily.

71 Emily. Sir surelie gif I vnderstude,
Zour meining for to be as gude,
I think in ane wee sould conclude,
    Befoir that it wer lang:
I am content to be zour wyfe,
To lufe and serue zow all my lyfe,
Bot rather slay me with a knyfe,
    Nor offer me ane wrang.

72 Bot sir, ane thing I haue to say,
My father hes this vther day,
In Mariage promisit me away,
    Upon ane deid auld man:
With quhome thocht I be not content,
Till nane vther he will consent,
Mak to thairfoir for till invent
    Ane convoy, gif zow can.

73 Lykewayis zow mon first to me sweir,
That ze to me sall do na deir,
Nor sall not cum my bodie neir,
    For villanie nor ill:
Ay quhill the Nuptiall day sall stand,
And farther sir, gif mee zour hand,
With me for to compleit the band,
    And promeis to fulfill.

74 Flavius. Haue thair my hand with al my hart
And faithfull promeis for my part,
Na tyme to change quhill deithis dart,
    Put till my lyfe ane end:
Bot be ane Husband traist and trew,
For na suspect that anis sall rew,
Bot readie ay to do my dew,
    And neuer till offend.

75 Emily. All day quhairto the treuth to tell,
I dar nocht with that matter mel,
Bot zit I fall deupfe my fell,
    Ane fchift to ferve our turne:
For keiping ftairt baith lait and air,
Unfend-furth may I neuer fair,
Make I ane mint and do na mair,
    I may for euer murne.

76 Quhen I haue vnbethocht me thryfe,
I can na better way deupfe,
Bot that I man me difagyfe,
    In habite of ane man:
Thus I but danger or but dout,
This bufines may bring about,
In mans array vnkend pas out,
    For ocht my keipars can.

77 Chairfoir ze fall gang and proupde,
Ane Pages claithis in the meine tyde,
For all occafions me befyde,
    Againft I haue ado:
Let me euin as thay lift me call,
Or quhat fumeuer me befall,
I hope within thrie dayis I fall,
    Cum quyetly zow to.

78 Flavius. Be my awin meins I fall atteine,
And fend to zow thay claithis vnfene,
Convoy lat fie all things fa cleine,
    That neuer nane fufpeck:
I will wait on my felf and meit zow,
To fe zour new claiths as thay fet zow,
The Carle that hecht fa weill to treit zow,
    I think fall get ane geck.
                  Emily

79 Emilie. I haue won narrowlie away,
Zon Carle half put me in effray,
he lay in wait and waiting ay,
    In changing aff my claithis:
Sir, let vs ga out of his ficht,
Sen I am frie, my freind gude-nicht,
he lukis as all things war not richt,
    Lo zonder quhair he gais.

80 Flavius. My onlie luif and Ladie quhyte,
My darling deir and my delyte,
how fall I euer the requyte,
    This grit gude will let fee:
That but refpect that men callis fchame,
Nor hazart of thy awin gude name,
For brute, for blafphemie nor blame
    hes venterit all for mee.

Stephano Albertus Servant.

81 Maifter full far I haue zow focht,
And full ill newes I haue zow brocht,
The thing allace, I neuer thocht,
    hes happinnit zow this day:
Zour douchter fir (ze had bot ane)
Ane mannis claithis hes on hir tane,
And quyetlie hes hir earand gane,
    I can not tell quhat way.

82 I wonderit firft and was agaft,
Bot quhen I faw that fho was paft,
I follouit efter wonder faft,
    Zit was I not the better:
Scho fchiftit hes hir felf afyde,
And in fum hous fho did hir hyde,
Na fir, quhat euer fall betyde,
    It will be hard to get her.
       D

83 Alberto. Fals pewtene hes scho playit that
Hes scho me handlit in this sort?   (sport
To God I vow cum I athort,
          And lay on hir my handis:
I sall hiz ane exampill mak,
To trumpers all durst vndertak,
For to commit sa foull ane fack,
          Quhill that this Citie standis.

84 Vplde vagabound, fals harlot hure,
Had sho na schame, tuke sho na cure,
Of parentis that hir gat and bure,
          Nor blude of quhilk sho sprang:
All honest bewtie to dispyse,
And lyke ane man hir disagyse,
Vnwomanlie in sik ane wyse,
          As gudget for to gang.

85 Fals mischant, full of all mischeif,
Dissaitfull traitour, commoun theif,
Of all thy kin curit not the greif,
          For fleschly foull delyte:
Quha sall into sik trumpers trust?
Quhais wickit wayis ar sa vnjust,
And led with lewd licentious lust,
          And beastlie appetyte.

86 Philotus. O sex vncertaine, frayle and fals,
Dissimulate and dissaitfull als,
With honie lips to hald in hals,
          Bot with ane wickit mynde:
Quhome will dois mair nor reasoun muse,
Mair lecherie nor honest luse,
Mair harlotrie nor gude behufe,
          Vnconstant and vnkynde.

PHILOTVS.

87 In quhome ane ſhaw, bot na ſhame ſinks,
That ane thing ſayis and vther thinks:
Ane eye lukis vp, ane vther winks,
  With fair and feinȝeit face:
Bot goſſop go, quhill it is greine,
Foȝ to ſeik out quha hes hir ſeine,
Gif of hir moyen wee get ane meine,
  It war ane happie grace.

88 Philerno. Gude ſirs, is nane of ȝow can tell,
In quhat ſtreit dois Alberto dwell,
Oȝ be quhat ſinge Ile knaw my ſell,
  Gude bȝethȝen all about:
Foȝ thocht I be his Sone and Heyȝe,
I knaw him not a myte the mair,
And to this Town dois now repair,
  My father to find out.

89 Alberto. Ȝea harlote, trowit thow foȝ to ſkip
Sen I haue gottin of the ane grip,
Be Chȝiſt I ſall thy nurture nip,
  Richt ſcharply oȝ wee ſched:
Foȝ God noȝ I rar in ane raip,
And euer thow fra my hand eſcaip,
Quhill I haue pullit the lyke ane Patp,
  Quhair nane ſall be to red.

90 Philotus. Rage not gude goſſe, bot hald ȝour
The las bot bairnlie is and ȝoung, (toung
I wald be laith to wit hir dung,
  Suppoſe ſcho hath offendit:
Foȝgiue hir this ane fault foȝ mee,
And I ſall ſouertie foȝ hir bee,
That inſtantly ſho ſall agree,
  That this ſlip ſould be mendit.
   D 2

91 Philerno. Father I grant my haill offence,
Thir claithes I haue tane till ga hence,
And gif it please zow till dispence,
    With thir things that ar past:
Thir bygane faultes will ze forgiue,
And efter father quhill I liue,
Agane I sall zow neuer greiue,
    Quhill that my lyfe may last.

92 Schaw me the maner and the way,
And I zour bidding sall obey,
And neuer sall zour will gane say,
    Bot be at zour command:
Alberto. This fault heir frelie I forgiue thee,
Philotus is the man releiues thee,
Or vtherwayis I had mischeifit thee,
    And now giue mee thy hand.

93 This is my ordinance and will,
Giue thy consent Philotus till,
To marie him and to fulfill,
    That godlie blissit band:
Philerno. Father, I hartlie am content,
And heirto giues my full consent,
For it richt sair wald mee repent,
    Gif I sould zow gainstand.

94 Philotus. Heir is my hand my darling dow,
To be ane faithfull spous to zow,
Now be my saull Gossop I trow,
    This is ane happie meiting:
This mater Gosse, is sa weill drest,
That all things ar cumde for the best,
Bot let vs set amang the rest,
    Ane day for all compleiting.

95 Alberto. Ane Moneth and na langer day,
For it requyres na grit delay,
Tak thair zour wyfe with zow away,
    And vſe hir as ze will:
Philotus. Forſuith ze ſall ga with me hame,
Quhair I ſall keip zow ſaif fra ſchame,
Unto the day, or than mee blame,
    That ſcho ſall haue nane ill.

96 Pleſant. Quha euer ſaw in all thair lyfe,
Twa cappit Cairlis mak ſik ane ſtryfe,
To tak a zoung man for his wyfe,
    Zon cadgell wald be glaid:
The feind reſaue the feckles frunt,
Put doun thy hand and graip hir cunt,
The Carle kennis not, he is ſa blunt,
    Gif ſcho be man or maid.

97 Auld guckis the mundie, ſho is a gillie,
Scho is a Colt-foill, not a fillie,
Scho wants a dow, bot hes a pillie,
    That will play the ane paſſe:
Put doun thy hand vane Carle and graip,
As thay had wont to cheis the Paip,
For thow hes gotten ane jolie jaip,
    In lykenes of ane Laſſe.

      Philotus ſpeiks to his Dochter Briſila.

98 Briſilla Dochter myne giue eir,
A Mother I haue brocht the heir,
To mee a wyfe and darling deir,
    I the command thairfoir
Hir honour, ſerue, obey and luif,
Wirk ay the beſt for hir behuif,
To pleis hir ſis thy pairt thow pruif,

With wit and all devoir.

Philotus to his new Bryde.

99 Vſe hir euen as zour awin my dow,
Keip hir, for ſho ſall ly with zow,
Quhill I may lawfullie avow,
    To lay zow be my ſyde:
Philerno. I ſall zour dochter husband ſweit,
Na les nor my companzeoun treit,
And follow baith at bed and meit,
    Quhill that I be ane bryde.

Philerno to Briſilla.

100 How dois the quheill of Fortoun go,
Quhat wickit weird hes wrocht our wo?
Briſilla zouris and myne alſo,
    Unhappilie, I ſay:
Our fathers baith hes done agrie,
That I to zouris, euin as ze ſie,
And ze to myne ſall marpit be,
    And all vpone ane day.

101 Hard is our hap and luckles chance,
Quha pities vs ſuppoſe wee pance?
Full oft this mater did I ſkance,
    Bot with my ſelf befoir:
I haue bene threatnit and forſittin,
Sa oft that I am with it bittin,
Invent a way or it be wittin,
    And remedie thairfoir.

102 Briſilla. Maiſtres allace for ſik remeid,
That ſik ane purpois ſould proceid,
I wald wiſch rather to be deid,
    Nor in that maner matchit:
Quhat aillit ze Parentes to prepair,

                                    zour

ʒour Childʒens deip continuall cair,
ʒour crewell handes quhy did ʒe spair,
   First vs to haue dispatchit.

103 Vnnaturall fathers now quhairfoir?
Wald ʒe ʒour dochters thus deuoir?
For ʒour vane fantasies far moir,
   Nor onie gude respeck:
Is it not doittrie hes ʒow dreuin,
Haiknapis to seik for haist to Heauin?
I trow that all the warld euin,
   Sall at ʒour guckrie geck.

104 Solace to seik themselues to sla,
Ane myʒe to misse thay fall in ma:
Thay get bot greif quhen as thay ga,
   To get thair greitest game:
And wee ʒoung things tormentit to,
Thairdassing dois vs swa vndo,
Gif thay be wyse, thair doings lo,
   Will signifie the same.

105 Philerno. It profeitis not for to compleine,
Let vs forsie ourselues betwene.
How wee this perrell may preueine,
   And saif vs fra thaiʒ snairis:
Gif that the Goddes, as thay weill can,
Wald mee transforme intill ane man,
Wee twa ourselues sould marie than,
   And saif vs fra thair cairis.

106 Brisilla. Mak ʒow a mã, that is bot mowis
To think thairon ʒour greif bot growis,
For that deuyse deuill haid it dowis,
   Sen it can neuer be:
Philerno. Quhy not? gif that with faith we pray

For oft the Goddes as I hard say,
Hes done the lyke and ȝit thay may,
    Perchance till vs agrie.

107 That Iphis was a Mayd we reid,
And swa did for hir prayer speid,
For verie reuth the Goddes indeid,
    Transformde hir in ane man:
Pigmaleons prayer purchaſt lyfe,
Unto his new eburneall wyfe,
Quhais handis had caruit hir with ane knyfe,
    With viſage paill and wan.

108 Quhy may not now als weill as than,
The Goddes convert me in ane man,
The lyke gif that my prayer can,
    I ſurelie will aſſay:
Maiſt ſecreit Goddes Celeſtiall,
Ȝe michtie Muiſers greit and ſmall,
And Heauinlie powers ane and all,
    Maiſt humblie I ȝow pray,

109 Luke doun from ȝour imppyre abone,
And from ȝour heich triumphant Trone,
Till us puir ſaullis ſend ſuccour ſone,
    Of ȝour maiſt ſpeciall grace:
Behald how wee puir Madynis murne,
For feir and luif how baith wee burne,
Thairfoir intill ane man mee turne,
    For till eſchew this race.

110 Behald our Parents hes oppreſt,
And by all dew thair Dochters dreſt,
With vnmeit matches to moleſt,
    Us ſillie ſaullis ȝe ſie:
Thairfoir immortall Goddes of grace,

                                    Grant

Grant that our prayeris may tak place,
Conuert my kynde, this cairfull care,
    With solace to supplie.

111 Plesant. Ane faith perfumit with fyne folie,
And monie vane word alla=volie,
Thy prayer is not half sa holie,
    House=lurdane as it semis:
Bot all inventit for a wyle,
Thy bedfallow for to begyle,
The bonie Lasse bot to defyle,
    Na dowbilnes that demes.

112 Brisilla. Maistris quhat now? bethink ʒe
Or than to be in sowne ʒe seime: (dreme,
Scho lyis als deid, quhat sall I deime,
    Of this vnhappie chance?
Scho will not heir me for na cryis,
For plucking on scho will not ryis,
Sa larbair-lyke lo as scho lyis,
    As raueist in a trance.

113 Philerno. O blissull Deitie diuyne,
Maist happie conuent, Court and Tryne,
That dois ʒour glorious eiris inclyne,
    Our prayeris to adheir:
We rander thanks vnto ʒow all,
For heiring vs quhen that wee call,
And ridding vs from bondage thrall,
    As plainlie dois appeir.

114 I am ane man Brisilla lo,
And with all necessaris thairto,
May all that onie man may do,
    I sall gar ʒow considder:
Now sen the Goddis abone hes brocht,
        E

Chis wonderous wark, and hes it wrocht,
And grantit all ruin as wee socht,
   Let vs be glaid togidder.

115 Britilla. Now seu the Gods hes succour sent
And done ruen as wee did invent,
My ioy I hartly am content,
   To do as ye deuyse:
Throw Gods deceit my onlie choyse,
In mutuall luif wee sall reiopse,
Our furious fathers baith suppose
   Thay wald skip in the Skyis.

116 Philotus. My dow suppois I did delay,
Now cum is our sweit Nuptiall day,
Thairfoir mak haist swa that wee may,
   In tyme cum to the kirk:
Philerno. Sa quhen ye list sir, I am readie,
Thair is ane Gas-breid, for be our Ladie,
I was your Sone, and ye my Dadie,
   This morning in the mirk.

117 Minister. I dout not bot ye understand,
How God is Authour of this band,
And the actioun that wee haue in hand,
   He did himself out set:
To that effect all men I meine,
Micht keip thair bodyes pure and cleine,
Fra Fornication till abstine,
   And Children to beget.

118 For sin the mater cums athort,
Ilk uther day, I will be schort,
And does the parteis baith exhort,
   To charitie and luif:
Tak heir this woman for your wyfe,

Keip, luif and cherisch hir but stryfe,
All vther als terme of zour lyfe,
    Saif hir ze sall remuif.

119 Tak for zour Spous Philotus than,
Obey and luif him as ze can,
Forsaik for him all vther man,
    Quhill deith do zow disseuer:
The Lord to sanctifie and blesse zow,
His grace and fauour als I wisch zow,
Let not his luif and mercie misse zow,
    Bot be with zow for euer.

Flavius conjuration.

120 O mercie God, how may this be?
Zon is indeid richt Emilie,
In forme of hir a faith I sie,
    Sum Deuill hes me defaisit:
I will in haist thairfoir gang hame,
Expell zon Spreit for sin and schame,
And to tell me the awin richt Name,
    For Gods caus I will craif it.

121 The Croce of God, our Sauiour sweit,
To saif and sane me fra that Spreit,
That thow na hap haue for to meit,
    With me in all thy lyfe:
In Gods behalf I charge the heir,
That thow straik in my hart na feir,
Bot pas thy way and do na deir,
    To neyther man nor wyfe.

122 First I conjure the be Sanct Marie,
Be Alrisch king and Queene of Farie,
And be the Trinitie to tarie,
    Quhill thow the treuth haue taull:
E 2

Be Chriſtand his Apoſtilles twell,
Be Sanctis of Heuin and hewis of Hell,
Be auld Sanct Caſtian him ſell,
 Be Peter and be Paull.

123 Be Mathew, Mark, be Luik and Johne,
Be Lethe, Stir and Acherone,
Be helliſche furies euerie one,
 Quhair Pluto is the Prince:
That thow depart and do na wonder,
Be lichtning, quhirle wind, hayle nor thunder,
That beaſt nor bodie get na blunder,
 Nor harme quhen thow gais hence.

124 Throw power I charge the of the Paip,
Thow neyther girne, gowl, glowme, nor gaip,
Lyke Anker ſaidell, like vnſell Aip,
 Lyke Owle nor Alriſche Elfe:
Lyke fyrie Dragon full of feir,
Lyke Warwolf, Lyon, Bull nor Beir,
Bot pas zow hence as thow come heir,
 In lykenes of thy ſelfe.

125 Emily. Gude-man quhat meine ze ocht bot
Quha hes zow put in ſik ane muder (gude
Befoir I neuer vnderſtude,
 The forme of zour conjuring:
Flavius. I charge the zit as of befoir,
Pas hence and troubill me no moir,
Crowis thow to draw me ouir the ſcoir,
 Fals feind with thy alluring.

126 Emily. Gude-man quhat miſteris all thir
As ze war cumbred with the cowis, (mowis?
Ze ar I think lyke Johne of Lowis,
 Or ane out of his mynde:
           Flavius.

Flavius. In Gods behalfe I the beseiche,
Impesche me not with word nor speiche,
Ill Spreit,to God I me beteiche,
    Fra the and al thy kynde.

127 Plesant. Ha ha,ha ha,ha ha,ha ha,
The feind resaue the lachters a,
Quhilk is the wysest of vs twa,
    Man quhidder thow or I?
Flemit fuill,hes thow not tint thy seill,
That takis thy wyfe to be ane Deill,
Thow is far vainest I wait weill,
    Speir at the standers by.

128 Flavius. I charge the zit as I haue ellis,
Be halie relickis,Beidis and Bellis,
Be Ermeitis that in desertis dwellis,
    Be Lumitoris and Carlochis:
Be sweit Sanct Steuin stanit to the deid,
And be Sanct Iohne his halie heid,
Be Merling,Rymour and be Beid,
    Be witchis and be warlochis.

129 Be Sanct Maloy,be Moyses Rod,
Be Mahomeit the Turkisch God,
Be Iulian and Sanct Elous nod,
    Be Bernard and be Bryde:
Be Michaell that the Dragon dang,
Be Gabriell and his auld sang,
Be Raphaell in tyme of thrang,
    That is to be as gyde.

130 Emily.My luif,I think it verie lyke,
That ze war Licht or Lunatyke,
Ze feir,ze frap,ze fidge,ze fyke,
    As with a Spreit possest:
      E 3

Quhat is the mater that ʒe mene?
Quhat garris ʒow braid?quhair haue ʒe bene?
Quhat aillis ʒow joy?quhat haue ʒe sene?
    To rage with sik vnrest?

131 Flavius. Quhat haue I sene fals hound of
I trowit quhen I did with the mell,   (Hell
Thow was richt Emilie thy sell,
    Not ane incarnate Deuill:
Bot I richt now with my awin Eine,
Richt Emilie haue marʒit seine,
Sa thow mon be ane Spreit vncleine,
    Lord saif me fra thy euill.

132 Be vertew of the halie Ghaist,
Depairt out of myne hous in haist,
And God quhais power and micht is maist,
    Conserue me fra thy cummer:
Gang hence to Hell or to the Farie,
With me thow may na langer tarie,
For quhy? I sweir the be Sanct Marie,
    Thou's be nane of my nummer.

133 Philerno. Gar wsche this hous for it grows
Husband I haue for to debait,   (lait
With ʒow a lytill of estait,
    Befoir wee go to bed:
Sen I am ʒoung and ʒe ar auld,
My curage kene,and ʒe bot cauld,
The ane mon to the vther fauld,
    A faith befoir we sched.

134 Philotus, We wil not for the maistrie
We mon grie better and we thryue,   (stryue,
Philerno. Na be my saull we'is wit belyue,
    Quha gets the vpper hand:
                    Indeid

Indeid thow fall beir mee a beuell,
For with my Neiues I fall the nauell,
Auld cuſtrone Carle tak thair a reuell,
    Than do as I command.

135 Philotus. I ſie it cummis to cuffis the man,
Ile end the play that thow began,
That victorie thow neuer wan,
    That fall be bocht ſa deir:
Ha mercie, mercie Emilie,
Tak ʒe the maiſtrie all for me,
For I fall at ʒour bidding be,
    And ſlay me not, I ſweir.

136 Pleſant. Wel clappit burd quhan wil ʒe kiſſe?
Auld fuill, the feind reſaue the miſſe,
Ʒe trowit to get ane burd of bliſſe,
    To haue ane of thir Maggies:
Quhat think ʒe now? how is the race,
Now ʒe'ill all doit, allace, allace,
Now grace and honour on that face,
    Quod Robein to the Haggies.

137 Philerno. Than hecht in haiſt thairfoir that
Sall readie at my bidding bow,   (thow
Quhat euer I do thow fall allow,
    My fanſie to fulfill:
Sa gang I out, ſa cum I in,
Sa gif I waiſt, ſa gif I win,
Quhat euer I do mak ʒe na din,
    Bot let me wirk my will.

138 Thou may not ſpeir the caus, & quhy,
Quhen that I liſt not with ʒow ly,
Quhat I the bid, and thow deny,
    Wee will not weill agrie:

Quhen that I pleis furth to repair
Speir not the cumpanie, noz quhair:
Content thy self and mak na mair.
    I man thy maister be.

139 Philotus. I am content quhen & how sone,
All till obey that ze insone,
That ze command it man be done
    Thair is nane vther buit:
Philerno. Quhat is zour pzyce Damesall fair?
Quhat tak ze foz a nichts lair?
Huir. Ze sall a Croun vpon me spair,
    Bot quhom with sall I do it?

140 Philerno. Ile get a man, haue heir a Croun,
Bot be weill strange quhen ze ly doun,
Mak nyce and gar the Larbair lowne,
    Beleue ze be a Mayd:
Huir. The zoungest Las in all this Citie,
Sall byde na mair requeist noz treitie,
Ile cry as I war huirt foz pitie,
    Quhen I am with him laid.

141 Emily. Now sen my Husband hes done sa
But caus foz to put me him fra,
I will vnto my father ga,
    Befoir his feit to fald:
Father sa far I did offend,
That I may not my mis amend,
And am ouir pert foz to pzetend
    Zour dochter to be cald.

142 Alberto. Lament not, let that mater be,
Thy faltis ar buriet all with me.
Betwixt thy Husband now and thee,
    Is onie new debait?

                         Emily.

Emily. I knaw of nane, bot hee indeid,
Hes put mee fra him, quhat remeid?
And will na mair sik fosteris feid,
    He sayis of myne estait?

143 Alberto. Quhat is the mater that ʒe meine
Against all ordour clair and cleine,
Schut hame ʒour wyfe that hes not bene,
    ʒit fyue dayes in ʒour aucht:
Is this ane plesant godlie lyfe,
To be in barrace, sturt and stryfe,
The feind wald faine man be ʒour wyfe,
    Can neuer sit in saucht.

144 Philotus. Knew ʒe the treuth gude-man I
Hir labour ʒe sould not allow,   (trow
Luke all my face, behald my brow,
    That is baith blak and bla:
Alberto. It may weill be, I can not tell,
That scho durst with that mater mell,
Let hir mak answer for hir sell,
    To sie gif it be sa.

145 Dochter gaue I the this command,
That thow thy husband sould ganestand,
How durst thow huir, him with thy hand,
    Put to the point of felling?
Emily. That war grit wrang sir, gif sa bee,
Bot hee na husband is to mee,
Than how could wee twa disagree,
    That neuer had na melling.

146 Alberto. Na melling Mistris? wil ʒe than
Deny the Mariage of that man,
In face of halie Kirk quha can,
    This open deid deny?

F

Emily. Let reſoun ſir with ʒow pꝛeuaill,
Condemne mee not firſt in the faill,
Befoir that ʒe haue hard my taill,
    The treuth ſyne may ʒe try.

147 Now this is all that I wald ſay,
That Flauius tuke mee away,
About a Moneth and a day,
    Dꝛeſt in a Uarlets weid:
With quhome I haue bene euer ſtill,
Ane vther Emilie ay and quhill,
Hee ſaw ʒow giue Philotus till,
    And than in verie deid,

148 Supponing mee ane Deuill of Hell,
With crewell conjuratiounes fell,
Did mee out of his hous expell,
    As with a Bogill baʒed:
As ane out of his mynde oꝛ marrit,
He hes mee of his hous debarrit,
I can not tell quhat hes him ſkarrit,
    Oꝛ hes the man amaʒed?

149 Alberto. This purpois goſſe, appeirs to me
Sa wonder nyce and ſtrange to be,
That wee to wit the veritie,
    Foꝛ Flauius man ſend:
Sir gif ʒe could declair vs now,
How lang this woman was with ʒow,
And all the maner quhen and how,
    Wee wald richt gladlie kend.

150 Flavius. Sa far Alberto as I knaw,
I ſall the ſuith vnto ʒow ſchaw,
Quhen I ʒour Douchters bewtie I ſaw,
    I offerit hir gude-will:
                  Accepting

Accepting than the promise maid,
Cled lyke a Boy but mair abaid,
Fra ȝow diſſaitfullie ſcho ſlaid,
    And come myne hous vntill.

151 Quhair I hir keipit as my wyfe,
Tret, luifit and chereiſt hir for lyfe,
Quhill efter-ward fell out ane ſtryfe,
    Thir maters all amang:
For plainlie in the Kirk I ſaw,
This man became ȝour Sone in law,
I did thairfoir perfytly knaw,
    My Emilie was wrang.

152 And that ſome Spreit hir ſchaip had tane
Sen Emilies thair was bot ane,
I thairfoir to that Ghaiſt haue gane,
    Conjuring hir my ſell:
And fra my hous expellit hir to,
This woman ſeimis for to be ſcho,
Senſyne I had na mair ado,
    With that fals feind of Hell.

153 Philotus. Now Flavius, I wait richt weil
Sen ane of them man be a Deill,
My maiglit face maks mee to feill,
    That myne man be the ſame:
For quhy? richt Emilie is ȝouris,
And that incarnate Deuill is ouris,
I gat, ȝe may ſie be my clouris,
    A Deill vnto my Dame.

154 Philerno. Heir I am cum to red the ſtryfe
For I am neyther Deill nor Wyfe,
Bot am ane ȝoung man be my lyfe,
    Ȝour Sone ſir, and ȝour Air.

Quhome ʒe foꝛ Emilie haif tane,
And wald not ſirs let mee allane,
Quhill ʒe ſaw quhat gait it is gane,
    I can tell ʒow na mair.

155 Philotus. A man,allace,and harmiſay,
That with my only Dochter lay,
Syne dang my ſell,quhat ſall I ſay?
    Of this vnhappie chance?
Haue I not maid a berrie block,
That hes foꝛ Jennie maryit Jock?
That mowit my Dochter foꝛ a mock,
    The Deuill be at the dance.

156 Allace,I am foꝛ euer ſchamit,
To be thus in my eild defamit,
My Dochter is not to be blamit,
    Foꝛ I had all the wyte:
Auld men is twyſe bairnis,I perſaif,
The wyſeſt will in wowing raif,
I foꝛ my labour with the laif,
    Am driuin to this diſpyte.

157 Alberto. Gude goſſe,ʒour wꝛaith to pacifie
Sen that thair may na better bee,
I am content my Sone that hee,
    Sall with ʒour Dochter Marie:
Philerno. I am content with hart and will,
This Mariage father to fulfill,
Quhat neidis Philotus to think ill,
    Oꝛ ʒit his weird to warie.

158 Flavius. Be frolick Flauius and faine,
To get thy Emilie againe
To deme my dow,was I not vaine,
    That thow had bene a Spꝛeit?

                      Now

Now sen I am fred fra that feir,
And vaine illusioun did appeir,
Welcum my darling and my deir,
    My sucker and my sweit.

159 Gude sirs, quhat is thair mair ado,
Ilk zouth his lufe hes gotten lo,
Let vs thairfoir go quicklie to,
    And marie with our maitis:
Let vs foure Lufers now rejoyse,
Ilk ane for to injoy his choyse,
Ane meiter matche nor ane of those,
    For tender zoung estaitis.

160 Let vs all foure now with ane sang,
With mirth and melodie amang,
Giue gloir to God that in this thrang,
    Hes bene all our relief:
That hes fra thraldome set vs frie,
And hes vs placit in sik degrie,
Ilk ane as hee wald wisch to be,
    With glaidnes for his greif.

Ane sang of the foure Lufearis.

WERE Jacobs Sones mair joyfull for to se,
The waltring wawes King Pharaois Dist
Was Israel mair glaid in hart to be (cōfound
Fred from all feir, befoir in bondage bound?
Quhen God thē brocht frō y͂ Egiptian ground,
Was Mordocheus merier nor wee,
Quhen Artacerxes alterit his decrie?

162 Was greiter glaidnes in the land of Greice
Quhen Jason come from Colchos hame agane,
And conquest had the famous golden Fleis,
With labour lang, with perrell and with pane?

The Father Æzon was not half sa faine,
To sie his Sone returning with sik gloir,
As wee, quhais myndis ar satisfyit, and moir.

163 Gif onie joy into this Earth belaw,
Or warldlie plesour reput be perfyte,
Quhat greiter solace sall ze to mee shaw,
Nor till injoy zour hartis all haill delyte?
To haue zour Lufe and lustie Ladie quhyte,
In quhome ze may baith nicht and day rejoyse:
In quhom eze may zour plesures all repose.

164 Let vs thairfoir, sen euin as we wald wisse,
Recipzocklie with leill and mutuall lufe,
As fleitand in the Fludes of joy and blisse,
With solace sing and sozrowes all remufe,
Let vs the fruttes of pzesent plesour pzufe,
In recompence of all our fozmer pane,
And miserie, quhairin wee did remane.

Philotus.

165. Bot now advert gude bzetherin all about,
That of my labour hes the succes seine:
Ze that hes hard this haill discourse thzowout,
May knaw how far that I abusit haue bene,
I grant indeid thair will na man me meine,
For I my self am authour of my greif,
That by my calling sould be carpit cleine,
With zouthlie topis vnto sa griet mischeif.

166 Gif I had weyit my grauitie and age,
Rememberit als my first and auncient sait,
I had not sowmit in sik vnkyndlie rage,
For to disgrace mine honour and estait,
Quhat had I bocht bot to my self debait,
Suppois the mater had run than as I meinit:

May

Nay my repentance is not half sa lait,
As I had gotin the thing quhairfoir I greinit.

167 For thocht my folie did the Lord offend,
Zit my gude God hes wrocht all for the best:
And this rebuik hes thairfoir to me send,
All sik inordinate doings to detest,
Quhilk sweit rebuik I reckin with the rest,
From fatherlie affection to proceid,
That vthers with lyke passiouns possest,
May leirne be my exampill to tak heid.

168 Sen age thairfoir suld gouernit be $\bar{w}$ skill
Let countenance accord with zour gray hairis
Ze auncients all, let resoun rewll zour will,
Subdew zour sensis till eschew thir snairis,
Gif ze wald not incombred be with cairis,
Be maister ouer zour awin affections haill:
For haillillie the praise is only thairs,
That may against sik passions preuaill.

The Messinger.

169 Gude sirs, now haue ze hard and sene this
Unworthie of zour audience I grant,   (ferse
Unformallie set out in vulgar verse,
Of waillit out words and leirnit leid bot skant
The Courteours that Princes hallis do hant,
I wait will neuer for my rudenes ruse mee:
Zit my gude-will for to supplie the want,
I hope sall of zour courtesies excuse mee.

170 For passing weil I haue imployit my panis
Swa that ze can be with the same content:
For dew regaird gude acceptiouns gaines,
And parties pleisit dois mak the tyme wel spět
Gif God had greiter leirning to mee lent,

Ĵ fuld haue fchawin the fame in als gude will:
Wlyte ignozance that Ĵ did not invent,
Ane ferſe that micht zour fantaſies fulfill.

171 Laſt ſirs, now let vs pzay with ane accozd,
Foz to pzeſerue the perſoun of our King:
Accounting ay this gift as of the Lozd,
Ane pzudent Pzince aboue vs for to ring.
Than gloir to God and pzayſis let vs ſing,
The Father, Sone and halie Gaiſt our gyde,
Of his mercies vs to conduct and bzing,
To heuin for ay, in pleſoures to abyde.

FINIS.

WHAT if a day or a month or a zeere
  Crown thy deſire with a thouſand wiſched contentings?
Can not the chance of ane nicht or ane houre,
Croſſe thy delightes with a thowſand ſad tormentings?
Fortune, honour, bewtie, zouth are but bloſſomes dying
Wanton pleſoures, dotting loue are but ſhadowes flying:
All our joyes are but toyes idle thoughtes deceauing,
None hes power of an houre in thair lyues bereauing.

  Earth's but a point of the World, and a man
Is but a poynt of the Earths compared centure.
Shall than the poynt of a poynt be ſo vaine
As to delight in a ſillie poynts aventure?
All is hazard that wee haue, here is nothing byding:
Dayes of pleaſures ar but ſtremes throgh fair medowes gly-
Well or wo tyme dois go, in tyme is no returning,   (ding
Secreete fates guydes our ſtates, both in mirth and murning.

  The Printer of this preſent Treatiſe hes (according to the
Kings Majeſties licence grantit to him) printit ſindrie vther
delectabill Diſcourſes vndernamit, ſic as are, Sir Dauid Lyn-
deſayis play, The Preiſtis of Pebles with merie Tailes, The
Freiris of Berwick, and Bilbo.

VARIOUS READINGS

IN THE EDITION OF 1612.

IN collating the two early editions of this Play, the following appear to be the principal variations ; the words of the edition of 1603 being first quoted, followed by the corresponding words of the edition of 1612.

The TITLE PAGE of Hart's edition has an Arabesque ornament at the top, with a shield in the centre, charged with the figure of a Heart interlaced with the letter A ;

LINE 1. 'Ane'—'A ;'

—— 2. 'Treatise,'—'Comedie ;'

—— 5. 'Fallis,'—'fall ;'

—— 8. 'Velis,'—'voles ;'

Andrew Hart's device, with A. H. below it, in place of Charteris' ; and the imprint, "EDINBURGH, Printed by Andro Hart, and are to be Solde at his Buith, on the North-side of the gate, a litle beneath the Crosse, ANNO DOM. 1612."

On the reverse of the Title—THE ARGUMENT. Philotus, an olde rich man, is enamoured with the loue of Emilia, daughter to Alberto, who being refused, imployeth a Macrell or Pandrous to allure her thereto, but all in vain ; afterward he dealeth with her father, Alberto, who being blinded with the man's wealth, vseth first faire words, and thereafter threatnings to perswade her thereto; the mayde still refuseth. In the mean time, Flavius, a young man, enters in conference with the Mayde, and obtaineth her consent, who, being disguised, conveyeth herselfe away priuilie with the said Flavius. Her father and Philotus searches for her in the house. Philerno, the Maydes brother, laitlie arryued out of other countries (being verie lyke her) is mistaken by her father and Philotus, to be Emilia, who takes the person of his sister vpon him : and after diuerse threatnings of his father, consenteth to marrie Philotus : and so Philotus committeth Philerno to the custodie of his daughter, Brisilla, vntill the mariage should be accomplished. Philerno faines himselfe to Brisilla, to be transformed in a man, and so maketh himselfe familiar with her. Thereafter, Philerno is maried to Philotus, who, fearing to be discouered, maketh a brawling that same night with Philotus, and abuseth him vyllie, and to colour the mater the better, agreeth with a whore to go to bed with Philotus. Flavius seeing the supposed Emilia to bee maried to Philotus, imagines the right Emilia to be a deuill, and, after many conjurations, expelleth her his house, she returneth to her father, Alberto, acknowledging her misbehaviour, and lamenting her case. Flavius being sent for, perceiuing how he had mistaken Emilia, reuealeth the whole trueth, and so taketh her home agane to his wife, and Philerno Brisilla. In the end Philotus bewaileth his follie for pursuing so vnequall a match, warning all men to beware, by his example.

LINE 1. ' Interlocutors,' ' Speakers.'
——13. ' Huir,' ' Whore.'
TITLE, l. 1. ' Ane,' ' A ;'
—————— l. 2. ' Treatise,' ' Comedie.'
St. II. v. 4. ' man,' ' must ;' 7. ' dow,' ' doue.' This word is sometimes printed *dow* in the edition of 1612, and sometimes altered to *doue*. The same remark will apply to *man* and *must ; gar* and *make*, &c.
St. III. v. 2. ' Ise,' ' Ile ;' 6. ' theirs,' ' the rer's.'
St. IV. v. 7. ' f ,' ' fucke.'
St. X. v. 2. ' Leise me thay,' ' Grace on these.'
St. XIII. v. 1. ' sen,' ' sith.'
St. XIV. v. 7. ' freine,' ' freind.'
St. XVI. v. 5. ' on,' ' in.'
St. XVIII. v. 3. ' and,' ' if ;' 5. ' birnand,' ' birning.'
St. XIX. v. 1. ' muilles,' ' mooles.'
St. XX. v. 1. ' the,' ' your ;' 8. ' not,' ' you.'
St. XXIII. v. 1. ' is,' ' are ;' 5. ' with,' ' of.'
St. XXVIII. v. 2. ' cheinzeis,' ' cheinies.'
St. XXIX. v. 5. ' stuffe,' ' stuste.'
St. XXXI. v. 6. ' rickillis,' ' heapes.'
St. XXXII. v. 6. ' nocht,' ' not ;' 7. ' neck me not with,' ' doe not say me.'
St. XXXIII. v. 1. ' rowan,' ' rowdan ;' 6. ' thay,' ' these ;' 8. ' thay,' ' these.'
St. XXXIV. v. 3. ' and,' ' an.'
St. XXXV. v. 7. ' heir,' ' may.'

St. xxxvi. v. 6. ' filthsum,' ' filthie ;' 8. ' sweit,' ' weit.'

St. xxxvii. v. 3. ' thir,' ' these.'

St. xxxviii. v. 1. ' care,' ' cure ;' ' cuit,' ' coote ;' 7. ' gar,' ' make.'

St. xlii. v. 7. ' thay,' ' the.'

St. xlvii. v. 8. ' man,' ' must.'

St. xlviii. v. 5. ' sen,' ' sith.'

St. l. v. 1. ' trumper,' ' strumpet ;' 2. ' was,' ' is ;' 6. ' gar,' ' make.'

St. lii. v. 2. ' off,' ' of.'

The lines printed in Roman letters at the end of Stanza liv. are omitted in the edition of 1612.

The word ' FLAVIUS' is inserted, in the edition of 1612, between the running-title and the first verse of Stanza lv.

St. lvi. v. 2. ' toistit,' ' tossed ;' 4. ' man,' ' must.'

St. lx. v. 3. ' clud,' ' cloud ;' 5. ' asse,' ' ashe ;' 7. ' nor,' ' then.'

St. lxi. v. 7. ' bwillis,' ' ballis.'

St. lxv. v. 1. ' Orisoun,' ' oration ;' 5. ' nocht,' ' no.'

St. lxviii. v. 3. ' word,' ' words.'

St. lxix. v. 1. ' Flavius,' ' Fla.;' 6. ' by,' ' for ;' 7. ' na,' ' not.'

St. lxxiv. v. 5. ' ane,' ' na ;' 6. ' anis,' ' once.'

St. lxxv. v. 5. ' stairt,' ' strait.'

St. lxxvi. v. 7. ' vnkend,' ' unknowne.'

St. lxxvii. v. 6. ' sumeuer,' ' soever.'

St. lxxviii. v. 6. ' as,' ' how.'

St. lxxxiii. v. 6. ' trumpers,' ' strumpets.'

St. lxxxiv. v. 4. ' quhilk,' ' whom.'

St. lxxxv. v. 3. ' curit,' ' caired ;' 5. ' trumpers,' ' strumpets.'

St. lxxxvii. v. 4. ' feinzeit,' ' fained.'

St. lxxxviii. v. 3. ' singe,' ' signe.'

St. lxxxix. v. 6. ' hand,' ' bands.'

St. xc. v. 8. ' sould,' ' shall.'

St. xci. v. 4. ' thir,' ' these ;' 5. ' thir,' ' these.'

St. xcii. v. 5. ' Alberto,' ' Alb.'

St. xciii. v. 5. ' Philerno,' ' Phil.'

St. xciv. v. 1. ' Philotus,' ' Phi.'

St. xcv. v. 1. ' Alberto,' ' Alb.'

St. xcvi. v. 1. ' Plesant,' ' Ple.;' 5. ' the,' ' your.'

St. xcvii. v. 2. ' colt-foill,' ' colt fool.'

St. xcviii. v. 8. ' all devoir,' ' indeuoure.'

St. XCIX. v. 5. ' Philerno,' ' Phil.'

St. CVI. v. 1. ' Brisilla,' ' Bri.'

St. CXI. v. 1. ' Plesant,' ' Ple.'

St. CXII. v. 1. ' bethink,' ' methink ;' 2. ' than,' ' els.'

St. CXIII. v. 1. ' blisful,' ' blessed ;' 4. ' to adheir,' ' for to heare.'

St. CXIV. v. 4. ' gar,' ' make.'

St. CXV. v. 1. ' Brisilla,' ' Bri.'

St. CXVII. v. 3. *dele* ' that.'

St. CXX. v. 3. ' a,' ' in.'

St. CXXI. v. 2. ' sane,' ' keepe ;' ' that,' ' thee.'

St. CXXII. v. 4. ' taull,' ' tauld ;' 7. ' Tastian,' ' Austian.'

St. CXXV. v. 1. ' Emily,' ' E. ;' 5. ' Flavius,' ' Fla.'

St. CXXVI. v. 1. ' Emily,' ' E.'

St. CXXX. v. 1. ' Emily,' ' Emi.'

St. CXXXI. v. 1. ' Flavius,' ' Fla.'

St. CXXXIII. v. 1. ' Philerno,' ' Philer. ;' ' gar wsche,' ' cause ush.'

St. CXXXIV. v. 1. ' Philotus,' ' Philot. ;' 3. ' Philerno,' ' Philer.'

St. CXXXV. v. 1. ' Philotus,' ' Phi.'

St. CXXXVI. v. 1. ' Plesant,' ' Ple. ;' 6. ' all doit,' ' do it all.'

St. CXXXVII. v. 1. ' Philerno,' ' Philer.'

St. CXXXIX. v. 1. ' Philotus,' ' Philo. ;' 5. ' Philerno,' ' Philer.'

St. CXL. v. 1. ' Philerno,' ' Philer. ;' 5. ' Huir,' ' Whore.'

St. CXLI. v. 1. ' Emily,' ' Em.'

St. CXLII. v. 1. ' Alberto,' ' Alber. ;' 5. ' Emily,' ' Em.'

St. CXLIII. v. 5. ' Alberto,' ' Alb. ;' 6. ' barrace,' ' barrate ;' 7. ' feind,' ' feiud.'

St. CXLIV. v. 1. ' Philotus,' ' Philo. ;' 5. ' Alberto,' ' Alb.'

St. CXLV. v. 3. ' huir,' ' whore.'

St. CXLVI. v. 8. ' syne,' ' then.'

St. CLII. v. 1. ' some,' ' her,' ' hir,' ' some ;' 3. ' haue,' ' hes.'

St. CLIII. v. 1. ' Philotus,' ' Philot.'

St. CLIV. v. 1. ' Philerno,' ' Philer.'

St. CLV. v. 1. ' Philotus,' ' Philo. ;' 4. ' chance,' ' chauce.'

St. CLVI. v. 5. ' is,' ' are.'

St. CLVII. v. 1. ' Alberto,' ' Alb. ;' 5. ' Philerno,' ' Philer. ;' 8. ' his,' ' this.'

St. CLVIII. v. 1. ' Flavius,' ' Fla.'

St. CLXIV. v. 3. ' fleitand,' ' fleiting.'

St. CLXVIII. v. 7. ' hailillie,' ' wholie all.'

St. CLXIX. v. 1. ' and sene this ferse,' ' vs here reherse ;' 4. ' leid bot,' ' language.'

St. CLXX. v. 3. 'acceptiouns gaines,' ' acceptance doth gaine ;' 8. ' Ane ferse,' ' And search.'

St. CLXXI. v. 1. ' Last, sirs, now let vs pray with ane accord,' ' Last, let vs pray to God with ane accord ;' 4. ' ring,' ' reigne.'

The poem, printed at the end of the play in the edition of 1603, is omitted in the edition of 1612.

APPENDIX;

CONTAINING

BARNABY RICH'S TALE

OF

PHYLOTUS AND EMELIA.

PHYLOTUS AND EMELIA.

[THE ARGUMENT OF THE VIII HISTORIE.

¶ Philotus, *an old and auncient Citizen of* Rome, *falleth in love with* Emelia, *a yong and beautifull virgin the Daughter of* Alberto, *who knowing the wonderfull wealth of* Phylotus, *would have forced his daughter to have married him; but in the ende was pretelie deceiued by* Phylerno, *the brother of* Emelia, *who married with* Phylotus *in his sisters stead, and other prety actions that fell out by the waye.*

It hath many times bin had in question, and yet could neuer be decided from whence this passion of extreame loue doth proceed, whose furie is such where it once taketh possession, that (as they say) loue is without law, so it maketh the Pacientes to be as utterly void of reason, but in my opinion the selfe same thing, which is many times shadowed under the title of loue, may more properly be termed, and called by the name of lust, but be it loue, or be it lust, the difference is nothing so much as the humour that feedes it, is wonderfull strange, and hath no maner of certainty in it, excepting this, it is without parciality, for commonly when it driueth us to effect, it is done without any maner of respect, for some time it maketh us to linger after our friends, sometimes to languish after our foes, yea, betweene whom there hath bin had mortall hostility : the sonne hath bin seene to fall in loue with the wife of his Father, the Father againe in like manner with the wife of his sonne, the King hath bin attached with the poore and needie begger, the poore againe in lyking with those of high degree, yea and though there haue bin many which

haue] seen their owne errour, and there withall haue confessed their abuse, yet
thei haue not bin able to refraine themselues, from prosecuting their follie
to the ende, and all be it, reason proffereth us sondrie sufficient causes, why
we ought to refraine the appetite of our own desires, yet fancie then is he
that striketh suche a stroke, that reasons rules can naught at all preuaile, and
like as those whom loue hath once intangled, the more thei striue the farther thei bee tied, so it is vnpossible that loue should be constrained, where
affection breedes not likyng, nor fancy is not fed, but where these two hath
once ioyned in election, all other affects be so dimme and blinded, that euery
vice seemeth to vs a vertue, whereof springeth this Prouerbe, In loue there
is no lacke, so that in deede to saie the truth, if there be any pietie to be
imputed to this ragyng loue, it is in that it is not parciall, nor hath it any
respect of persons, but bee thei frendes, be thei foes, be thei riche, be thei
poore, be thei young, be thei olde, bee thei wise, bee thei foolishe, loue is
still indifferent, and respecteth all a like : but if any man will thinke that in
respect of beautie, wee esteeme not all the rest : I am able to saie it is not
true, consideryng how many haue forsaken the better likyng, and haue
chosen the worse, so that for my parte the more I consider of it, the more
I am amazed, and therefore will beate [my braines no more about it, but leave
it to the credit of such as have bin louers themselves, whose skil in the
matter I preferre before mine owne, and will come to my Historie of Phylotus, who being an aged man, fell in loue with a yong maiden, farre unfit-
ting to his yeares, and followeth in this sort.

In the gallant citty of Naples, there was remaining a young man, called
by the name of Alberto. This Alberto beeing married not fully out a yeere,
his wife was deliuered of a Sonne whom he named Phylerno, and upon diuers
considerations, minding to chaunge his habitiation, he prepared himselfe to
goe dwell at Rome, and first taking order for his sonne Phylerno, who for the
tendernesse of his age he left still in Naples at nurse, himselfe, his wife, with
all the reste of his household came to Rome, where he had not long remained,]
but his wife was likewise deliuered of a daughter, whom he called by the
name of Emelia, who as she grewe in yeares, she likewise proued to bee

very beautifull and faire, and amongst a greate nomber of others, there was dwellyng in Rome an auncient Citizen, whose name was Phylotus, a man very orderly in yeares, and wonderfully aboundyng in goodes, this Phylotus hauing many tymes taken the viewe of Emelia, beganne to growe very sore in loue with her, or rather I maie saie in his olde yeares beganne to doate after this young maiden, for it can not bee properly called loue in these olde men, whose dotage if it were not more then outragious, either their greate discretion would represse it, either their many yeares would mortifie it. But Phylotus in the ende desired Emelia of her father in the waie of Mariage, Alberto accordyng to the custome of Parentes, that desires to marrie their daughters, more for goods, then for good will betweene the parties, more for lucre then for loue, more for liuing then for learning, more for wealth then for wit, more for honour then for honestie, and so thei maie haue great store of money thei neuer consider farther of the man. Alberto in like maner knowyng the wealth wherewith Phylotus was indued, who had neuer a childe but one onely Daughter, whose name was Brisilla, gaue his full consent, without any farther consideration of the inequalitie [of the yeares that was betweene Phylotus and his daughter: he neuer remembred what strifes, what iarres, what debates, what discontentment, what counterfaiting, what dissembling, what louring, what loathing, what neuer liking, is euer had where there is such differences betweene the married, for perfect loue can neuer be without equalitie, and better were a married couple to continue without liuing, then without loue: and what are the occasions that make so many women to stray from their husbands, but when they be married to such as they cannot like of: but surely if women did throughly consider how dangerous it is for them to deale with these olde youthes, I thinke they would be better aduised in medling with them, for besides that they be unwildie, lothsome, (and, sir, reuerence of you,) very unlouely for you to lye by, so they be] commonly inspired with the spirite of Jelousie, and then thei will looke to you so narrowly, and mewe you vp so closely, that you will wishe a thousande tymes the Priest had bin hanged that maried you, but then to late.

But to retourne to our Historie: Alberto respectyng more the wealth of
Phylotus, then the likyng of his daughter, gaue his consent to take hym for
his sonne in lawe, and told Emelia how he had disposed on her: Emelia
seyng what an olde babie her father had chosen to be her housebande, moste
humbly desired hym to giue her leaue to choose for her self, whereat her
father being very angrie, beganne sharply to rate her, saiyng: And arte
thou then so muche wedded to thine owne will, that thou skornest to be de-
rected by me thy louyng father, or thinkest thou that thy wisedome doeth
so farre surmount my wit, that thou canst better prouide for thy self, then
I whiche so carefully haue hetherto brought thee vp, or doeth the tender
loue or the chargeable cost whiche I haue bestowed on thee, deserue no better recompence, then to despise those that I would haue thee to like of.

Emelia fallyng doune of her knees before her father saied: Moste deare
and louyng father, moste humbly I beseech you, for the affection whiche by
nature you beare me, not to think me so gracelesse a childe, that I would
goe about to contrarie you, or stubbornly would refuse what soeuer you
would think conuenient for my behoofe, and although you shall finde in me
suche duetie as is meete for a daughter, and al obedience that is fit for a
childe, yet sir consider the harte whiche can not bee compelled, neither by
feare, neither by force, nor is not otherwise to be lured, then onely by
fancies free consent, and as you haue bestowed on me this fraile and transi-
torie life, so my bodie shall be at your disposition as it shal please you to
appoint it, and will conclude with this humble petition, desiryng you not to
bestowe me of any that is not agreeable to my fancie and good likyng.

Well (quoth her father) then see you frame your liking to like well of my
likyng. I haue promised you to Phylotus in mariage, and Phylotus is he
that shall be your housband, and looke you goe not aboute to contende
against that I haue determined, if you doe, neuer accompt me for father nor
freende, and thus he departed.

Emelia hearyng this cruell conclusion of her father, was wonderfully
abashed, and beeyng by her self in her Chamber, she beganne to consider of

her fathers wordes, and for feare to incurre any farther displeasure, she deused how she might frame her self to the likyng of her louer, and with a yong womans minde, she first beganne to consider of his wealth, of his call-yng, of the reuerence wherewith he was vsed in the Citie, and that likewise in beyng his wife, she should also bee had in estimation, and bee preferred before other women of meaner credite, and to desire superioritie, it is com-monly euery womans sicknesse, and therefore this could not choose but please her very well : then she remembered how commodious it were to marrie one so wealthie as Phylotus, whereby she should not neede to beate her braines aboute the practising of housewiferie, but should haue seruauntes at com-maundment to supplie that tourne, this likewise pleased her very well, but be-cause she would well perswade her self, she beganne to coniecture how she should spende the tyme to her contentment, and therefore she beganne to thinke what a pleasure it was to bee well furnished with sondrie sutes of ap-parell, that in the mornyng when she should rise, she might call for what she list to put on, accordyng as the tyme and the fasshion did require, and her fancie serued best, for thus Phylotus was well able to keepe his wife, and this pleased her likewise very well, & then when she were vp, she might breake her fast with a cuppe of Malmsie, or Muskadine next her harte. It was very good for ill Ayres in a mornyng, and this she thought was but an easie matter, and likewise pleased her very well : when she had broken her fast, then she might stirre about the house, and looke to this, and see to that, and where she found any thyng amis, not to touche it with her owne fingers, for marryng the beautie of her hande, but to call for Cicelie, Ione, or Cate, and to chide them like Sluttes, that thei could not spie a fault but when thei must be tolde : this likewise pleased her very well, then to haue prouided for Dinner some iuncketts, that serued best her appetite, her housbāde had good store of coine, and how could it bee better spente, then vpon themselues : to make their fare the better, this likewise pleased her verie well, now when she had dined, then she might goe seeke out her examplers, and to peruse whiche woorke would doe beste in a Ruffe, whiche in a Gorget, whiche in a

Sleeue, whiche in a Quaife, whiche in a Caule, whiche in a Handkercheef, what Lace would doe beste to edge it, what seame, what stitche, what cut, what gard, and to sit her doune, and take it forthe by little and little : and thus with her Nedle to passe the after noone, with deuising of thinges for her owne wearyng, this likewise pleased her passyng well : Then to prouide for Supper some shift of diet, and sondrie sauces, the better to help the stomacke, Oranges, Lemōs, Oliues, Caphers, Salades of sondrie sortes, alas a Croune will goe a greate waie in suche trifles. This likewise pleased her verie well, whē she had supped, to vse some exercise, accordyng to the ceason : if it were in Sommer, to goe walke with her neighbours to take the aire, or in her Gardein to take the verdure of sweete and pleasaunt flower, this likewise pleased her verie well, when she was come in, and readie to goe to her Chamber, a Cup of cold Sacke to bedward, is verie good for digestion, and no coste to speake of, where suche abondaunce doeth remaine, and this likewise pleased her verie well.

But now although she had deuised, to passe the daie tyme with suche contentation, when she remembred at Night, she must goe to bed to bee lubber leapt : and with what cold courtesie she should be entertained by her graie hedded bedfelowe, what frosen embracementes he was able to bestowe of her, all was marde, and quite dashte out of remembraunce, and all the commodities before spoken of, that she should receiue in the tyme of the daie, would not serue to counteruaile that one incommoditie, in the season of the Night : Like as wee saie, one vice spilles a greate nomber of vertues. Thus Emelia was now to seeke, and could in nowise frame her self to loue Philotus : but when she had flattered her self with a thousande delightes, that she should receiue in the daie time by his wealth, when she remembred bedde tyme, she was as newe to beginne as before. Wherefore she remained in great perplexitie, thinkyng her happe to bee ouer hard, and the comforte verie bare, where the beste choice had suche assuraunce of doubtfull ende. For to Marrie after her Fathers mynde, she knewe would breede her lothed life : and to gainsaie what he had determined, would likewise loose her fathers

likyng, that she wiste not for her life whereon to resolue, and thus from daie
to daie, as she continued in this doubt ; there happened to hit into her companie a yong Romaine gentleman, whose name was Flanius, who sodainly
fell in Loue with Emelia, and takyng the tyme whilest his oportunitie
serued, he let Emelia to vnderstande, of the greate loue he bare her.   Emelia, accordyng to the custome of women, made the matter verie coie at the
firste, although in her harte she wer right glad, cōsideryng her case how it
stood.   Flanius was so muche the more importunate vppon her, and with
suche nice termes as woers be accustomed : He so Courted, and followed
Emelia, that she perceiuyng his feruente affection, tolde hym a verie short
circumstaunce, how her father had disposed her, to one that she could not
like of, and therfore, if he would firste promise to take her as his wife, and
that he could finde suche meanes, to conueigh her from her Fathers house in
secrete sorte (for otherwise she was sure her Father would bee a let to hinder
their purpose) she was contented to harken to his speeche, and yeeld to his
demaunde.   Flanius the gladdest man in the world, to heare these ioyfull
newes, sware vnto her, that all should bee accomplished, and that with as
muche speede as her self would desire.

There was no more to conclude of thē, but how she might be conueighed
from out her fathers house.   Flanius deuised that late in an Euenyng, or in
the Night tyme when euery one were quiete in their beddes, if she could
finde the meanes to gette forthe of doores, then he would be readie to receiue
her.   But that could not be, for bothe her Father and Mather neuer failed,
to bee at home in the Euenynges, and at Nightes she was lodged in her Fathers Chambers, that it was impossible for her to gett forthe.   So that there
was no remedie, but that the feate must bee wrought in some after Noone,
when bothe her Father and Mother vsed to bee abroade, about their busi-
nesse : And then she knewe not how to come forthe alone, because she had
not been accustomed so to dooe, and to followe a straunger, it would breede
the greater suspition.

But Flanius to auoide all these surmises, deuised the nexte euenyng to

conueigh her in at some backe windowe of her fathers house, a sute of
apparell : wherin the next daie in the after noone, her father & mo
yng abrood, she should shift herself, and so come her waies vnknowne
to suche a place : where he himself would be ready awaiting for her
conueigh her home to his owne house. This deuise Emelia liked
well, and accordyng as it was appoincted, the next euening Fla
neighed this sute of apparell in at the windowe, where Emelia w
to receiue it, and laiyng it vp in safetie, til the next daie in the afte
her father and her mother beyng bothe forthe of dores, she quickl
her self, into this manes apparell, and thus forth of dores she goes t
pointed place, where Flauius was staiyng, who accordyng to prom
neighed her home to his owne house.

This matter was not so closely handeled by Emelia, but she was
one of her Fathers seruauntes, who beeyng on the backside through
dowe, sawe her how she was stripping of her self, and marked how
on the manes apparell, whereat the yong fellowe had greate mer
stoode still beholdyng to see what would fall out in the ende. Bu
sawe her goe forthe a dores, he hastened after into the streate : Bu
was so sodainly gone, that for his life he wist not whiche waies to se
her, wherfore in a woderfull haste, he came to his Maister, whom h
in the Citee, in the companie of Philotus, saiyng : Oh sir, I haue v
newes to tell you, what is the matter (q. his maister) is any thyng a
home : Yea sir (q. the seruaunte) your daughter Emelia is euen no
ed into the citee, in the habite of a man : But whiche waies she
could not for my life deuise, for after she gat once forthe of the pl
she shifter her, I could neuer more set eye of her.

Is Emelia gone (quoth her louer Philotus) Oh God, what euill n
these that I heare : And without any further staie, bothe the Fa
the Louer, gat them out at the doores together, and aboute the str
runne like a couple of madde men.

Now it fell out, that Philerno the Sonne of Alberto, and B

Emelia, whom you haue heard before, was lefte at Naples, beeyng an Infante, and had remained there till this tyme at Schoole, and at this verie instaunte was come from Naples to Rome, to visite his Father and Mother, of whom he had no maner of knowledge, otherwise then by their names. And it fortuned that Alberto and Philotus, happened to meete with Philerno in the streates, who was so like his sister Emelia, that bothe Alberto and Philotus, assured themselues, that it could bee no other but she. Wherefore Alberto commyng to hym, saied: staie, staie, moste shamelesse and vngracious Girle, doest thou thinke that by thy disguising of thy self, in this maner, thou canst escape vnknowne to me, who am thy Father, Ah vile strumpet that thou art: what punishement is sufficient for the filthinesse of thy facte: And with this he seemed, as though he would haue fline vpon her in the streate, to haue beate her: but Philotus thruste in betweene them, and desired his neighbour to staie hymself, and then imbracyng Philerno in his armes, he saied: Ah Emelia my sweete and louing wenche, how canste thou so vnkindelie forsake thy Philotus, whose tender loue towardes thee is suche, that as I will not let to make thee soueraigne of my self, so thou shalt be Dame and Mistresse of all that euer I haue, assuryng thee, that thou shalt neuer want for Golde, Gemmes, Jewelles, suche as bee fit and conuenient for thy degree.

Philerno seeyng a couple of old dotyng foole thus clusteryng aboute hym, not knowyng what thei were: had thought at the first, thei had been out of their wittes, but in the ende by their woordes, perceiuyng a farther circumstance in the matter, he deuised some thyng for his owne disporte, to feede them a little with their owne follie, saied: Pardon me I beseeche you this my greeuous offence, wherein I knowe I haue too farre straied from the limites and boundes of modestie, protestyng hereafter so to gouerne my self, that there shall bee no sufficient cause, whereby to accuse me of suche vnmaidenlike partes, and will euer remaine with suche duetie and obediēce, as I trust shall not deserue but to be liked duryng life.

Philotus hauyng heard this pitifull reconciliation, made by his Emelia,

I

verie gently entreated her father, in her behalf, well (q. her father) seeyng
you will needes haue me to forgiue this her leudnesse, at your requeste I am
contented to pardon her, and then speakyng to Philerno, he saied :

How saie you houswife, is your stomacke yet come doune, are you contented to take Philotus for your Housebande, yea my good Father (q. Philerno) and that with all my harte, Oh happie newes (q. Philotus) and here
withall he began to sette his cappe on the one side, and to turne up his mus-
chatoes, and fell to wipyng of his mouthe, as though he would haue falne
a kissyng of her by and by in the streates, but remēbryng hym self where
he was, he brought Alberto with Philerno, into a freendes house, that was
of his familiare acquaintaunce, and there the Marriage betweene theim was
throughlie concluded, and all parties seemyng to giue their full consentes.
Philotus desired his father in Lawe, that he might haue the custodie of
Emelia, swearing by his old honestie, that he would not otherwise vse her,
then his owne Daughter Brisilla, vntill the daie of his Nuptials, and then to
vse her as his wife : to which request Alberto seemed verie willynglie to giue
consent : but then because Philotus would not carrie his beloued, through
the streates in her mannes apparell, he desired his Father in Lawe to goe
home, and sende some sute of her apparell, wherwith to shift her, before he
would carrie her to his owne house.   Alberto seyng matters so throughly
concluded, toke his leaue of theim bothe, and goyng his waies home, he
caused all his Daughters apparell to be looked together, and to bee sent to
the place where Philotus was remaining with Philerno, who taking forthe
suche as should serue the tourne for that present, Philerno so well as he
could arraied hymself, in one of his sisters sutes of apparell, and thus departed with Philotus to his owne house, where Philotus callyng his daughter Brisilla, he saied vnto her, beholde here the partie, whom I haue chosen
to bee your Mother, chargyng you of my blessyng, that you honour, reuerence, and obeie her, and with all diligence that you be attendaunt vpon her,
and readie at an ynche to prouide her of any thing, that she shall either want
or call for.   And you my deare and louyng Emelia, I dooe here ordaine and

appoincte you to bee Mistresse of this house, and of all that is in it, desiryng
you to accepte of this my Daughter, to doe you seruice in the daie time,
and in the night to vouchsafe her for your bedfellowe, vntill our daie of
Marriage bee prefixed, and then my self will supplie the rome. Philerno
seyng the excellent beautie of Brisilla, was nothyng sorie to haue suche a
bedfellowe, but thought euery hower a daie, till night was come, whiche
beyng approched, to bedde thei went, where Philerno did not thinke it his
readiest waie to giue any sodaine attempte, but therefore he brake into this
discourse followyng.

My Brisilla, were it not but that wee bee founde parciall in the causes of
our frendes, but especially where the causes doe touche our parentes, our
iudgementes be so blinded by affection, that we can neither see, nor well confesse a manifest truth: but if matters might be considered on, without respect of persones with indifference, and accordyng to the truthe and equitie
of the cause: I durst then put my self in your arbitremente my Brisilla, and
to abide your sentence, whereto I doubte not, but you would confesse the
preiudice I sustaine, it is muche intollerable, and almoste impossible, for a
yong maide to endure, and the rather, if you would measure my condition,
by your owne estate, who beeyng as you see, a yong maiden like your self,
and should be thus constrained by my freendes, to the mariyng of your father, whom I doe confesse to bee worthie of a better wife then my self. But
consideryng the inequalitie of our yeres, I cannot for my life, frame my self
to loue him, and yet I am forced against my will to Marrie hym, and am
appointed to be your mother: that am more meete to be your cōpanion and
plaie fellowe. But that affiaunce whiche I haue conceiued in your good
Nature, hath made me thus boldly to speake unto you, desiryng but to heare
your opinion with indifferencie, whether you thinke I haue good cause to
cōplain or naie: and then peraduenture I will saie farther vnto you, in a
matter that doeth concerne your owne behoofe.

Brisilla hearyng this pitifull complaint, verie sorrowfull in her behalfe,
saied: would to God I were as well able to minister releef vnto your dis-

tresse, accordyng to your owne contentment, as I am hartely sorie to consider your greef, and do well perceiue the iuste occasion you haue to complaine.

Ah my Brisilla, saied Philerno, I am as hartely sorie in your behalf, and peraduenture doe vnderstande somethyng, whiche your self dooe not yet knowe of, whiche will greeue you verie sore. But first Brisilla, let me aske you this question, dooe you knowe my father, or naie.

No sure (quoth Brisilla) I haue no maner of knowledge of hym, neither did I knowe, whether you had any father aliue, or naie, but now by your owne reporte, and as straunge it was to me, to heare the wordes, whiche my Father vsed to me this daie, when he brought you home, for that I neuer vnderstoode before, that he went about a wife.

Philerno was verie glad to heare these newes, because it serued so muche the better for his purpose : and therefore saied as followeth.

This tale that I minde to tell you (my Brisilla) will seeme more straunge then all the reste, and yet assure your self, it is nothyng so straunge as true, and therefore giue eare to that I mynde to saie : Doe you not thinke it verie straunge in deede, that the one of vs should bee made bothe mother and daughter to the other, and that our fathers, whiche be now so diescrepit and olde, should bee so ouer haled, with the furie of their fonde and vnbrideled affections, that to serue their owne appetites, thei force not with what ologges of care, thei comber vs that be their louyng daughters, but haue concluded betwene them selues a crosse Marriage, and so in deede it maie well be tearmed, that will fall out so ouerthwarte to our behoofes, who beyng now in our yong and tender yeres, and should bothe of vs bee made the dearlynges of twoo old men, that seekes to preferre their owne lust, before their childrens loue, and measure their fierie flames of youth, by the ded coles of age, as though thei were able with their cold and rare imbracementes, to delaie the forces of the fleshe, whose flames doeth excede in these our grene and tender yeres, and as muche possible for vs to cōtinue in likyng, as flowers are seen to agree with Froste, but in plaine tearmes (my Brisilla) and to discipher a verie trothe, it is contracted betweene our aged parentes, that your father (as you see) should first take me to his wife, whiche wedᵈdyng beyng once performed, then my Father in like maner, should chalenge you, accordyng as it is concluded betweene them.

Alas (q. Brisilla) these newes bee straunge indeede, and it should seem by your woordes so fullie resolued on, that there is no hope of redresse to be had in the matter.

None in the worlde (q. Philerno) but thus betweene ourselues, the one of vs to comfort the other.

A colde comforte (q. Brisilla) wee shall finde in that, but oh pitilesse parentes, that will preferre your own pleasures with your childrens paine : your owne likyng, with your childrens loathyng : your owne gaine, with your childrens greefe : your owne sporte, with your childrens spoile : your owne delight, with your childrens despight. O how muche more happie had it been, that we had neuer been borne.

Alas my Brisilla (q. Philerno) tormente not your self with suche exᵗtreame anguishe, for if that would haue serued for redresse, the matter had been remedied, and that long sithence : But I would to God my Brisilla, that I were a man for your only sake, and hauing so good leisure, as thus beyng together by our selues, we should so handle the matter, that our faᵗthers should seeke newe wiues.

Alas (q. Brisilla) suche wishes are but waste, and vnpossible it is, that any suche thing should happen.

Impossible (quoth Philerno) naie surely Brisilla, there is nothing imposᵗsible, but I haue knowne as greate matters as these haue been wrought : Doe we not read that the Goddesse Venus, transformed an Iuorie Image, to a liuely and perfect woman, at the onelie request of Pygmalion. Diana likewise conuerted Acteon to a Harte. Narcissus for his pride was turned to a flower. Archane to a Spider, with a greate number of others haue bin transformed, some into Beastes, some into Foules, and some into Fishes, but amongst the rest of the miracles that haue bin wrought by the Goddesse, this storie falleth out moste meete and fittyng to our purpose.

There was sometime remainyng in the Countrey of Phestos a maried couple, the housbande called by the name of Lictus, the wife Telethusa, who beyng with childe, was willed by her housbande so sone as she should be deliuered, if it were not a lad, that the childe should presently be slaine, his wife beyng deliuered at her appointed tyme, brought forthe a girle, and yet notwithstandyng her housbandes commaundement, brought vp the childe, makyng her housebande beleeve it was a boye, and called it by the name of Iphis, and thus as it grew in yeares, was apparelled like a lad, and beeyng after by his father assured to a wife called by the name of Ianthe, a young Maiden, and the daughter of one Telest dwellyng in Dictis, Telethusa the mother of Iphis, fearyng her deceipt would bee knowne, deferred of the Marriage daie so long as she could, sometymes fainyng tokens of ill successe, sometimes faining sicknesse, sometymes one thyng, sometymes an other, but when all her shiftes were driuen to an ende, and the Mariage daie at hande, Telethusa comming to the Temple of the Goddesse Isis, with her heire scattered aboute her eares, where before the Aulter of Isis, she made her humble supplications, and the gentle Goddesse hauing compassion, transformed Iphis to a man.

Loe here Brisilla, as greate a matter brought to passe as any wee haue spoken of yet, and the Goddesse bee of as greate force and might in these daies, as euer thei were in times past, we want but the same zeale and faith to demaunde it, and sure in my opinion, if either of vs made our request to the Goddes, who commonly bee still assistant to helpe distressed wightes, thei would neuer refuse to graunt our reasonable requestes, and I will aduenture on it my self, and that without any farther circumstaunce.

And here with all he seemed, with many piteous sighes, throwyng vp his handes to the heauens, to mumble forth many woordes in secrete, as though he had beene in some greate contemplation, and sodainly, without any maner of stirryng either of hande or foote, did lye still as it had been a thyng im-

mouable, whereat Brisilla beganne for to muse, and in the end spake to
hym, but Phylerno made no maner of aunswere, but seemed as though he
had bin in some traunce, wherewith Brisilla began to call and with her arme
to shake him, and Phylerno giuyng a piteous sigh, as though he had bin
awaked sodainly out of some dreame, saied, O blessed Goddesse Venus, I
yeeld thee humble thankes, that hast not despised to graunt my request;
and then speakyng to Brisilla, he saied : and now my Brisilla be of good
comforte, for the same Goddesse whiche haue not disdained to heare my
supplication, will likewise be assistaunt to further our farther pretences, as
hereafter at our better leisure we shall consider of, in the meane tyme receiue thy louyng freende, that to daie was appoincted to bee thy fathers
wife, but now consecrated by the Goddesse to be thy louyng housbande;
and here withall imbrasyng Brisilla in his armes, she perceiued in deede
that Emelia was perfectly metamorphosed, which contented her very well,
thinkyng her self a thrise happie woman to light of suche a bedfellowe : thus
bothe of them the one pleased very well with the other, thei passed the
tyme, till Phylotus had prepared and made all thinges readie for his Mariage
daie, and then callyng his frendes and neighbours about him, to the Churche
thei goe together, where Alberto gaue Phylerno his sonne, in the steede of
his daughter Emelia to Phylotus for his wife : when all the rest of the
Mariage rites that are to bee doen in the Churche were performed, thei passed
forthe the daie with feastyng and great mirthe vntill it was night. When the
companie beganne to breake vp, and euery one to take his leaue, and Phylotus with his bride were brought into their Chamber, where Phylerno desiryng the companie to auoyde, and makyng fast the doore he saied to Phylotus, there resteth yet a matter to bee decided betweene you and me, and
seyng we bee here together by our selues, and that tyme and place doeth fall
out so fit, I hold it for the best that it be presently determined.

What is the matter then (q. Phylotus) speake boldly my Emelia, and if
there be any thyng that hanges in dispence betweene vs, I trust it shall
easely bee brought to a good agreement.

I praie God it maie (q. Phylerno) and to reueale the matter in breefe and shorte circumstaunce, it is this. You are now my housebande, and I your lawfull wife, and for that I dooe knowe the difference in our yeares, your self beyng so old and I very yong, it must needes fall out there wil be as greate deuersitie in our conditions; for age is commonly giuen to bee frowarde, testie, and ouerthwart : youth againe to be frolique, pleasaunt, and merrie, and so likewise in all our other conditions wee shall bee founde so contrary and disagreyng, that it will be impossible for vs to like the one of the others doinges, for when I shall seeme to followe my owne humour, then it will fall out to your discontentment. And you againe to followe that diet whiche your age doeth constraine, will be most lothsome vnto me, then you beyng my housbande will thinke to commaunde me, and I must be obedient to your will, but I beyng your wife will thinke scorne to be controlde, and wil dispose of my self according to my owne liking, and then what braules and brabbles will fall out, it were to muche to be rehearsed, and thus we shall liue neither of vs bothe in quiet, nor neither of vs bothe contented, and therefore for the auoidyng of these inconueniences, I haue deuised this waie, that beyng thus together by our selues, we will trie by the eares whiche of vs shall bee maister and haue authoritie to commaunde : if the victory happen on your side, I am contented for euer after to frame my self to your ordinaunce and will as it shall please you to appoinct : if otherwise the conquest happen on my side, I will triumph like a Uictor, and will looke to beare suche a swaie, that I will not be contraried in any thing, what so euer it shall please me to commaunde.

Phylotus knowyng not what to make of these speeches, and thinkyng the tyme very long, till he had taken his first fruites, saied : Come, come my Emelia let vs goe to bed, where I doubt not but we shall so well agree, that these matters wil easely be taken vp, without any controuersie, suche as you haue spoken of.

Neuer while I liue (q. Phylerno) before I knowe whereon to resolue; and whether you shall rest at my commaundement, or I at yours.

Why (q. Phylotus) doe you speake in earnest, or would you looke to commaunde me that am your housbande, to whom you ought to vse all duetie and obedience.

Then were I in good case (q. Phylerno) that should be tied to vse duetie or obedience to a man of your yeares, that would not let to prescribe vs rules of your owne dotage, to be obserued in steede of domesticall discipline.

Then I perceiue (q. Phylotus) wee shall haue somethyng adoe with you hereafter, that will vse me with these tearmes the very first night. But see you make no more to dooe, but come on your waies to bed.

And I perceiue (quoth Phylerno) the longer that I beare with you, the more foole I shall finde you; and with this vp with his fiste and gaue Phylotus a sure wheritte on the eare. Phylotus, in a great rage, flies againe to Phylerno: there was between them souse for souse, and boxe for boxe, that it was harde to Judge who should haue the victorie. In the ende Phylerno gettes Phylotus faste by the graie bearde, and by plaine force pulles him doune on the flower, and so be pomels hym aboute the face, that he was like to haue been strangled with his owne bloud, which gushed out of his nose and mouth. Wherefore, holdynge vp his handes, he cried, Oh Emelia, I yeeld my self vanquished and ouercome; for Gods sake holde thy handes, and I will neuer more contende with thee during life.

Phylerno, staiyng hymself, saied: Art thou contented then to yeeld me the conquest, and hereafter this according as thou hast saied: neuermore to striue with me, neuer to gainsaie any thyng, what soeuer it shall please me to commaunde.

Neuer while I liue (q. Phylotus) and therefore for Gods sake let me arise, and chalenge to your self what superioritie you please, whiche for me shall neuer be denaied so long as I shall liue.

Well (q. Phylerno) but before I will let you arise, I will haue you promise me to confirme these conditions, whiche folowe in this maner. First, that at my pleasure, I maie goe abroade with my freendes, to make merrie

K

so often as I list, whither I list, and with whom I list. And neither at my goyng forthe, to be demaunded whither I will, ne at my returne to bee asked where I have been. I will farther haue you condescende to this, that forasmuche as I haue learned, that it is not onely very vntothsome, but likewise very vnwholesome, for youth and age to lye sokyng together in one bedde, I will therefore make no bedfellowe of you, but at my owne pleasure. And in maner as followeth, that is to saie: this first yere I shall be contented to bestowe one night in a moneth to doe you pleasure, if I maie see you worthie of it, or that you bee able to deserue it: but the first yere beyng once expired, fower tymes a yeere maie very well suffice, that is one night a quarter, as it shall please myself to appoinct. There be many other matters whiche I will not now stande to repeate, but these before rehearsed, bee the principall thynges wherein I wil not be controlde, but meane to follow myne owne liking: How saie you Phylotus, can you bee contented to frame yourself herein, to followe my direction.

Alas (quoth Phylotus) I see no other shift, I must perforce endeuour my self paciently to abide what soeuer it shall please you to commaunde, and doe yeeld myself as recreant, and ouercome, and wholy doe put my self to your fauour and mercie, readie to receiue what soeuer it shall please you to awarde vnto me.

Phylerno, letting hym now arise, saied: prepare your self then to goe to your bedde, and anon, at myne owne leasure, I will come vnto you; and departe againe at myne owne pleasure, when I shall see tyme.

Phylotus, comforting hymself with these sweete speeches, did thinke it yet to be some part of amendes, that she had promised to come and visite hym: went quietly to his bedde, there to abide the good hower till Emelia did come.

Phylerno, hauyng prepared one of these marcenarie women (whereof there are greate store in Rome to bee had) conueighed her to the bedd of Phylotus, giuyng her enstructions how to vse her selfe: and went hymself to his best beloued Brisilla, whom he had made priuie to his whole deuise; and in this maner it was agreed betweene them, thei had thought to haue dieted Phylotus once a moneth with some cast stuffe, suche as thei could hire best cheape in the Toune.

But it fell out that Flanius, whom you haue heard before, had stolne awaie Emelia, beyng at the Churche the same daie that Phylotus was maried, and sawe Alberto giue his daughter Emelia to Phylotus for his wife : had thought assuredly that hymself had been deceiued by some Deuill or spirite, that had taken vpon hym the likenesse of Emelia. And, therefore, hastyng hymself home with all possible speede, came to Emelia, and blessing him-self, he saied : I charge thee in the name of the liuyng GOD, that thou tell me what thou art, and that thou presently departe to the place from whence thou camest. And I conjure thee in the name of the Holie Trini-tie, by our blessed Ladie the Virgine Marie, by Aungels and Archaungels Patriarkes and Prophetes, by the Apostles, and fower Euangelistes, Mat-thewe, Marke, Luke and Jhon, by al the holie Martyres and Confessours, and the rest of the rable and blessed route of Heauen, that thou quietly de-parte without any maner of preiudice, either to man, woman, or childe, either to any maner of beast that is vppon the face of the earth, the Foules of the ayre, or the Fishes of the Sea, and without any maner of Tempest, Storme, Whirle winde, Thunder or Lightnyng, and that thou take no maner of shape, that maie seeme either terrible or fearfull vnto me.

Emelia hearyng these wordes, merueilyng muche what thei ment, with a smilyng countenaunce came towardes Flanius, saiyng : Why how now, Seig-nior Flanius, what doe you thinke me to be some Deuill, or any Hagge of Hell, that you fall so to Coniuryng and blessyng of your self?

I charge thee come no nere (quoth Flanius) stand backe, for these intice-mentes can no longer abuse me, when I haue seen with myne eyes, my be-loued Emelia, maried in the Churche, and giuen by Alberto her Father, to Phylotus for his wife, what should I thinke of thee but to be some Feend, or sent vnto me by some Inchauntment or Witchcraft; and therefore I will no longer neither of thy companie, neither of thy conference: And here withall

takyng Emelia by the shoulders, he thrust her forthe of doores, and shut-
tyng the doore after her: He gat hym to his Chamber, where he fell to his
praiers, thinkyng assuredly that Emelia had been some spirite.

But Emelia, after she had a three or fower daies made what meanes she
could to Flanius, and sawe it was in vaine, was driuen to goe to her Father,
before whom fallyng vppon her knees, she desired hym moste humbly to forgiue her.

Alberto takyng her vp in his armes saied: that he knewe nothyng wherein she had offended hym, but her suite might easily be graunted.

Deare father (quoth Emelia) I know I haue offended, and so farr as my
fact deserueth, rather to be punished than pitied: the remembraunce whereof is so lothsome vnto me, that I feare to call you by the name of father,
hauing shewed my self so vnworthie a daughter. These wordes she pro-
nounced with such sorrowe, that the teares streamed doune her cheekes;
wherewith Alberto, moued with natural affection, said: Deare child, I
knowe no suche offence that ought to bee so greeuously taken; but speake
boldly, whatsoeuer it be, I freely forgiue it.

Emelia very well comforted with these speeches, beganne to discourse how
she first disguised herself in Page's apparell, and what greef it was to her
conscience, that she should so farr straie from the duetie and obedience of a
child, and to become a fugitiue in a man's apparell. But her father not
sufferyng her further to proceede in her tale, saied: Alas, deare daughter
if this bee the matter, it is long agoe sithe I haue bothe forgiuen and for-
gotten these causes: and therefore let these thynges neuer trouble you. But
tell me nowe how doe you lik of your bedfellowe? how agree you with hym,
or he with you, I would be glad to knowe?

Alas deare father (quoth Emelia) that is the matter that I come to you,
he hath turned me awaie, and wil no longer take me for his wife, and what
is the cause that hath moued hym vnto it I protest before God I knowe
not for my life.

Hath he turned thee awaie (q. Alberto) my self wil quickly find a re-

medie for that matter, and without any more to do, (would not tary so much
as while his goune was a brushing) but out of doores he goes towards Phylotus, whom by chaunce he met withall in the Streates, and in a greate chafe
begins to chalenge hym for abusyng of his daughter, swearyng that he would
make all Rome to speake of his abuse, if he ment to proceede in that he had
begunne.

Phylotus, wonderyng to see the man in suche an agonie, beganne to wishe
that he had neuer seene hym nor his daughter neither, and that if any bodie
haue cause to complaine it is I (quoth Phylotus) that haue maried such a
wife, that is more like to a deuill then a woman ; and I perceiue now is
maintained in her mischiefe by you that are her father, who ought rather to
rebuke her then so to take her part, and to incourage her in her leudenesse.

What incouragment is this you speake of (q. Alberto) I knowe not what
you meane by these wordes ; but assure your self of this, that as I wil not
maintaine my child in any thing that is euill, so I will not see her take a
manifest wrong.

Doe you thinke this to be good then (quoth Phylotus) that your daughter should bestowe suche hansell on her housband as she hath alreadie bestowed vpon me, and then pointyng to his face, he saied : See here your
daughter's handie woorke, how thinke you, is this requisite to be borne with
all, that you stande so muche in your daughter's defence ?

Alberto seeyng his face all swolne, and the skinne scratched of, perceiued
that Phylotus was at a fraie, and had good cause to complaine : And wonderyng
that his daughter was so sodainly become a shrewe, saied : If this bee my
daughter's handie woorke, I can neither beare withall, neither will I allowe
it in her, so to vse her housebande. And therefore I praie you, lette me heare
the matter debated betweene you ; and I doubt not, but to take suche order,
as there shall no more any suche rule happen betweene you.

I am contented you shall debate what you will (q. Phylotus) so it
maie be doen with quietnesse, but I will neuer more contende with her for

(q. Alberto) here commeth the other Emelia, wee shall now trie, whiche of them is the Deuill (I thinke) before we departe.

By this Philerno was come in, and hearyng how matters had been debated, and were falne out : againe, knowing Alberto to be his Father, and what preiudice his sister Emelia was like to sustaine, if she should be forsaken by her freende and louer Flanius, confessed the whole matter, humblie desiryng his Father to forgiue hym.

When he had a while wondered at the circumstaunce, and the truthe of euery thyng laied open, and come to light, all parties were well pleased and contented, sauyng Philotus, for when he remembred, first the losse of his loue Emelia, then how Philerno had beaten hym, what a bedfellowe he had prouided hym, while he hym self went and laie with his daughter; these thinges put all together, made hym in suche a chafe, that he was like to runne out of his wittes. But when he had regarded a good while, and sawe how little helpe it did preuaile hym, he was contented in the ende that his daughter Brisilla, should Marrie with Philerno, and Flanius verie ioyfully receiued againe his Emelia (when he knewe she was no Deuill,) and bothe the Marriages consummate in one daie.

And so I praie God giue them ioye, and euery old dotarde so good successe as had Philotus.

FINIS.

CPSIA information can be obtained at www.ICGtesting.com
Printed in the USA
LVOW01s2317200315

431398LV00032B/2557/P